Conversations
in the Wings

Conversations in the Wings

TALKING ABOUT ACTING

Roy Harris

—— WITH ——

STOCKARD CHANNING

CHARLES DURNING

VICTOR GARBER

JULIE HARRIS

MADELINE KAHN

TERRY KINNEY

MARCIA JEAN KURTZ

ROBERT SEAN LEONARD

S. EPATHA MERKERSON

CYNTHIA NIXON

ROGER REES

RON RIFKIN

SAB SHIMONO

Foreword by Wendy Wasserstein
and André Bishop

HEINEMANN
PORTSMOUTH, NH

Heinemann
A division of Reed Elsevier Inc.
361 Hanover Street
Portsmouth, NH 03801-3912

Offices and agents throughout the world

Library of Congress Cataloging-in-Publication Data

Conversations in the wings : talking about acting / Roy Harris.
p. cm.
ISBN 0-435-08638-3
1. Actors—United States—Interviews. 2. Acting. 3. Theater.
I. Harris, Roy.
PN2285.C59 1994
792'.028—dc20 93-46703
CIP
Cover photograph by Robert Karosis.
Text and cover design by Gwen Frankfeldt
Printed in the United States of America on acid-free paper
97 96 95 94 HP 1 2 3 4 5 6

Contents

Contents

Acknowledgments

I will probably never by able to thank sufficiently the actors who allowed me to have these conversations. Most particularly, thanks to Terry Kinney, Robert Sean Leonard, Ron Rifkin, Julie Harris, Stockard Channing, and Roger Rees, who did interviews before I had a publisher. But I thank all thirteen for their generosity and for being artists whose work has given me that feeling of wonder I've cherished so many times— whether in the audience, in the rehearsal hall, or in the wings.

I also thank Playwrights Horizons, specifically for the use of both the Studio Theatre and the Mainstage for several interviews; the Mark Taper Forum, too, for interview space; Lincoln Center Theater, whose staff, including Julia Judge, Ed Nelson, Mari Eckroate, and Patrick Herold, was greatly useful in helping to arrange and expedite several interviews. To Daniel Swee, who through his wonderful casting connections made possible several interviews; Philip Rinaldi; Janet Foster; Helene Davis; the late Charlie Willard; Betty Travitsky of the Billy Rose Collection at Lincoln Center Library for the Performing Arts; Erica Tener; Marc Thibodeau; Dale Isaacs; Susan Chicoine; Don Scardino; Jody Milano; Jack Doulin; Reagan Fletcher of the Shubert Archive; Larry Katen; Sylvia Morris of the Shakespeare Centre Library; Jane Seiler; Elise-Ann Konstantin; Carol Fishman, and David Milligan—all for reasons they know, I hope.

And finally, my great and heartfelt thanks to Wendy Wasserstein and André Bishop, first for their Foreword, but really for a more important thing: being true friends of the American theatre.

Foreword

What makes a good stage manager? Efficiency, organizational ability, congeniality, unflappability, knowledge of technical aspects of theatre, energy and devotion, calm under fire, and an effortless ability to announce "Ladies and Gentlemen, it's half-hour, half-hour to curtain" on the backstage monitor, night after night after night.

What makes a *great* stage manager? All of the above plus a love of theatre and, most especially, a love of actors. Roy Harris is a great stage manager, and because he loves and understands actors he is uniquely suited to be the author of this book.

Roy will only stage manage first-rate shows. He has an unerring instinct for signing himself up to work on the best projects by the best writers, directed by the best directors, and with the best casts. And once a director or actor works with Roy, he or she always wants to work with him again.

The actors in this book of interviews—from the comic genius that is Madeline Kahn to the intensely cerebral Ron Rifkin—are all artists of quality and accomplishment. Most of all, they are creatures of the theatre. And a great stage manager such as Roy Harris *understands* his actors, just as a great interviewer must understand his subject.

Nobody knows more about creating the perfect atmosphere for actors to pursue the deeply complicated excellence of their craft than a production stage manager. In this book, Roy Harris has created a relaxed, informal atmosphere in which actors feel free to talk about the mysteries and intimacies of acting. We salute Roy and commend this book to you.

Wendy Wasserstein
André Bishop
Lincoln Center Theater

Preface

It was early November 1988, a rehearsal space on 42nd Street in New York City. Joan Allen (who was playing Heidi) and Peter Friedman (who was playing Scoop) were about to do a run-through of Act I, scene 2, of Wendy Wasserstein's *The Heidi Chronicles:* the "McCarthy for President" fundraising dance, which is their first meeting and the beginning of a relationship that will last for twenty years. For several weeks of rehearsal, these two actors had been diligently working on the scene. Joan, a brilliantly instinctive actress, takes whatever she's given by another actor and incorporates it into her performance; in rehearsal, she's almost completely malleable. Peter, a richly and intricately methodical actor, brings ideas into rehearsal he has carefully worked out at home; he'll agonize over a moment until it's completely filled. So far the scene wasn't working. Everyone knew it.

They started. Heidi, looking puzzled and somewhat frightened, entered and crossed to the punch bowl. Scoop followed and, as he reached around her for a handful of potato chips, said, "Are you guarding the chips?" "No," she replied. "Then you're being very difficult." The scene began to play. Within a few seconds, we were completely caught up in the attraction and clash of these two people. We laughed and couldn't take our eyes off of them. Joan and Peter were working together, and it was thrilling.

That rehearsal was the genesis of this book. Two completely different ways of working had fused. And I never forgot it.

The formal idea for a book, however, did not occur to me for two more years. It was late summer 1990, and I was talking with a friend about Terry Kinney's performance as the lapsed preacher Jim Casy in the Steppenwolf Theatre Company's production of *The Grapes of Wrath*.

I had just seen the show for the second time and was, again, moved by it and by Terry's work. Was the performance, as I suspected (and having worked with Terry twice, I felt I had the edge here), basically a triumph of instinctive acting? Or, as my friend felt, was it carefully crafted, thus very *theatrical?* "You know," I said suddenly, "Someone should do a book of interviews with actors about their technique." "What do you mean?" my friend said. "Well, a really thorough look at the way, say, ten working actors approach different roles." My friend, knowing my longtime interest in the subject, looked at me and asked, "Why don't you?"

I think I know a lot about acting technique, and from a layman's point of view, I suppose I do. Over a number of years, I have watched scores of actors work on a wide variety of roles, in different plays, and in various acting styles. But what a revelation these interviews for *Conversations in the Wings* have been. The first one took place on January 2, 1991 (and, not surprisingly, it was with Terry Kinney). The last one—with Madeline Kahn—on June 11, 1993. In these two-and-a-half years, my notion of technique has changed radically. It is so much broader and more encompassing than I ever suspected. Technique, I have learned, really has no boundaries. It is everything that goes on in an actor's mind (and how it shows in the body) from the first time he reads the script to the last time he says that character's words. "It's an ongoing process," Madeline Kahn said to me in her interview, "from the moment I know I'm going to be doing it until well after the reviews are out and I'm sure I know what it is. And it never stops."

Much has been said about technique—some of it useful, a great deal of it pompous and somewhat pretentious, and a lot of it said by people who've never been on a stage. *Conversations in the Wings* is a chance for actors to speak for themselves. The questions asked in each interview are meant to be an outline, a means of organizing the subject so there's a basis for comparison between one person's way of working and another's. The questions were designed to cover the acting process from the first time a script is read, through the prerehearsal work, the rehearsals themselves, the relation with the director and other actors, the opening and the reviews, to the final performance.

The actors interviewed here were very carefully chosen. They are primarily stage actors, but all of them work in film and television, too.

My major criterion: each had to be an actor whose stage work I admired—a lot. I love good acting. Very few things in this world move me as much as watching one person become another person. And when I experience this phenomenon at its deepest, I always have a sense of wonder, sometimes awe. Every person interviewed here has moved me this way more than once.

In choosing the actors in this book, I also tried for as much diversity as possible. I wanted a rich combination of seasoned performers and those early in their careers, well-known and relatively unknown, and as much variety of background, education, and actual acting experience as possible. For specifics about each actor's career, there are biographies at the end of the book. Their purpose is to give an overall view of each actor's work and to serve as a reference to the interview itself. They are, in no way, meant to be complete.

The interviews themselves: They were each about an hour-and-a-half in length. They were tape recorded, transcribed verbatim, and then edited. I have tried to retain in the editing the casual, relaxed feeling that the interviews actually had. Here and there you will find some unusual grammar, and its intention is to maintain the "conversational" quality.

Some people, as you will see, talk more coherently about how they work than others. To some people, technique is very conscious. One of the biggest lessons I learned from these interviews is that a lot of acting technique is unconscious. In fact, two different actors, after reading the edited versions of their interviews, told me that they did not know that they knew some things until they said them.

The important theme here, though, is of the interrelationships among the different ways of working. Who, for instance, researches a role? Who doesn't? Why? Who does major work on the script before rehearsal? Who waits until rehearsals begin? What are the different ways of approaching an accent? Which actors feel they need to know early in rehearsal what they will be wearing (and, consequently, may bring into rehearsal clothes to work with)? Which actors feel their character's background is critical, and what are the different ways of discovering what that background is? What kinds of homework are done? Who does extensive homework? Who relies more on the rehearsal process itself? What are the different ways of learning lines? Which actors want a strong director who is constantly pushing? Which ones want to be left alone? The samenesses and differences among the various approaches represented in these interviews are what make them not only fascinating, but wonderfully enlightening.

This book is meant to dispel the myth that if you talk about acting—and this was said to me by an actor who turned down an interview—"It will lose all its mystery." I look at the information in the thirteen interviews here, and acting has never seemed both more grounded and, at the same time, more magical and mysterious.

Roy Harris

Conversations
in the Wings

Delineating a Character

CHARLES DURNING

This interview took place in the living room of Mr. Durning's Wilshire Boulevard apartment in Los Angeles on Saturday, January 9, 1993. The night before he had taped an episode of his television series *Evening Shade*, and though he said he was tired, you would never have known it from the energy with which he spoke about acting. The person who, in his own words, had "no formal training" talks about his craft in a way that is wonderfully human, and that makes it easily accessible, even to a layman. Mr. Durning approaches every aspect of his career with the same energy and concentration: two days later he went on location in North Carolina to appear in a new film by Joel and Ethan Coen, *The Hudsucker Proxy*.

Roy Harris: When you read a script and say, "I've got to do this role," what makes you feel that?

Charles Durning: In the beginning of my career, which is going back a ways now, I'd take anything at all. I never had the luxury of saying, 'I'm not going to do this part because I don't like the character.' I just wanted to work so I'd do it. My feeling was, "You've got a part. I'll show up for rehearsal." There's no role at the moment that I want to do, but if I see a part (and we're talking about plays now) that I'm absolutely wild about, it's usually because something happens to the character to change him, and it moves me. Also, there's something universal in its approach. Something changes the other people in the show and maybe even will change the opinions of the people in the audience. A play like *Death of a Salesman*, or *Streetcar Named Desire*, or *King Lear* does.

RH: Interesting that you mention that because when you said there were no parts you wanted to play, I thought, "He should play Lear."

CD: Oh, really! Well, I've been asked to, but it's not right yet. Maybe later when I get very old, or very much older.

RH: Well, I know your Boss Finley in *Sweet Bird of Youth* from our working together. And I loved your performance as Big Daddy. What made you want to do him? Of course, it's a great role.

CD: I have seen Big Daddy many times, and I never liked what I saw. Even the original. I thought he was a force, a presence. But he never moved me. I felt there was something else in Big Daddy. Now when I started unpeeling it and getting down into the lower levels of it, I realized that there was. Nobody knew what it was except the director and me—we discussed it. I wouldn't even tell the actor playing Brick because I wasn't sure he could handle it.

RH: Would you discuss it now?

CD: What I felt was that Big Daddy may have been involved in homosexual activities himself. It's in what he says to Brick, "I've seen everything. I've done everything. I can appreciate it if you are." He lived with these two men who raised him, his surrogate fathers. They left everything to him. Why? He had been on his own since he was ten. He saw things, and I felt he had a moralistic point of view that was never shown. For instance, he never cheated on his wife though he hated her.

RH: This is fascinating.

CD: Now most people would disagree with that version of Big Daddy.

RH: Well, I had no idea what was inside you, but you made me feel about him for the first time. And isn't that why we go to the theatre, to feel?

4

CD: Of course. It should be as if you're peeking through a keyhole, seeing the intimacies of human feeling. If you don't have that, then you're not seeing good theatre.

RH: When you get the role and you're going into rehearsal in two weeks, say, what sort of work do you do beforehand?

"A play is like a puzzle you're trying to find the proper piece to. You fit it and you know when it's right. You may be struggling, but you know, even unconsciously sometimes, when it's right."

CD: First, I read the play over and over. Just read it, and I pick out certain passages that I like and I look them over. Now I've never had any real formal training as an actor, so I don't know what the process is. I actually started acting in 1948. I've read in newspapers that I didn't get my first professional job until 1962. I don't know where they got that, but maybe that's when they first started noticing me. But it was '48. Before that I worked in burlesque, then as a singer and dancer. I even worked with Alvin Ailey. Alvin later worked as an actor, and I used to say to him, "You know, you are to acting what I am to dancing."

Anyway, because I've had no real training, I've found my own way, and my form of studying is to study the other characters first. I see who my character is through the other people around him. And then I look at what he points out about himself and if it gels with the other characters. He may be lying, you know; and if he is, that's important. And then I create a backstory: who am I? where did I come from? what's my life out of this play like? who is my family? what was the early life like? Now, nobody knows this story but me.

It always dismays me when I hear young actors say in rehearsal, "Well, why does he do this?" because that's all homework to me. I don't need two weeks before the rehearsals. I need three months. I'm not a quick

5

study. When I come to the first rehearsal, I like to have everything memorized because the book in my hand and the words not in my head hinder me. I can't create until the book is out of my hand.

Now some actors will say that they won't learn the lines until they're in rehearsal—it stiffens them to learn them first. But I learn them in what I call a loose way, so that if somebody changes something I can change too. But I'm able to change with the flow *because* I know the lines. If I didn't know them, I'd feel things were going too fast for me. The same thing with stage business. If you get some business down on your own, and the director says, "Well, what if you did this?" you should be flexible enough to go with whatever the changes are. If I know the lines beforehand, I can.

RH: Would you say that you are more an instinctive actor or one more given to plan?

CD: I'm definitely more an instinctive actor. If you say something to me, I can react to that. Every question you ask, I'm responding to at this moment. I need someone to bounce off of. If I'm not getting it, I create it for myself. But, you know, I very seldom deviate once something is set. (I don't improv in performances unless someone else does something, and then I may *retaliate*, as they say.) But I don't like improv in performance, I like it all structured. For me, structured is better than unstructured.

RH: When you're in rehearsal, and let's say it's now the third day and you're going to work on Act I, scene 3, what do you do the night before to prepare for the next day's work?

CD: I don't really plan anything. I just read the whole thing. I read the play every single day, even during performances. I come to the theatre at least an hour before I'm called to go over the play before each performance.

RH: I remember because your dressing room was right next to my office in Toronto.

CD: But I do it from the back to the front, rather than front to back because when you start at the back and go to the front, you are prepared to go forward. If you're at the end of the play, you may be in a down

6

mood and it may be wrong to start that way—you'd be in a different mood from the way the play begins.

RH: When you're in rehearsal, what are you looking for from other actors? What's a good rehearsal situation for you?

CD: Mainly honesty. Even if they're going up on their lines. If the honesty is there, if the depth of character is there, or partially there (and you can see that it's going to come), then that excites me. A play is like a puzzle you're trying to find the proper piece to. You fit it and you know when it's right. You may be struggling, but you know, even unconsciously sometimes, when it's right.

There are various tricks that I use as I study. If I'm struggling with a certain passage, I pretend that the audience or the director or the person I'm talking to is a child, and I'm trying to explain it to him. When you explain something to a child, you understand it better yourself. In rehearsal, of course, you can't do all of this floundering—this is for home. Another trick is pretending that nobody in the audience can speak English. That helps you find various ways of getting the thoughts across. If you can't speak the language, then what do you do?

RH: What is a good rehearsal situation that you were in, one you remember with pleasure?

CD: Everything I did with Joe Papp at the Public. I was there from the beginning, the very first season. I was there for eleven years. It was a wonderful experience. Well, I've been very fortunate. I've been in some really wonderful companies. I've also been in some that made me wish I could swim ashore. That's another thing, you know: acting can be compared to being adrift in a lifeboat in the middle of an ocean. Everybody is suspicious in the beginning. Everybody has different ideas. Everybody wants to put in their own thoughts and ideas about what direction we should go. Eventually, we are all pulling in the same direction and heading for shore. But up until everyone is focussed on the same idea, it's chaos.

RH: What's a rehearsal situation that you found really unbearable?

CD: Well, I've been in those, and it was too much for me. On one I gave my notice a week before the show opened, and we knew it was going to be a pretty big hit. But I just couldn't take the people in it—too many egos. The leads used the other actors as props. It was awful.

RH: What are you looking for in rehearsal from a director?

CD: He's got to have an idea even if it's only the germ of one. He can't say to me, "Let me see what you've got." Because, frankly, I don't know what I've got. And really I don't want to hear a director say, "Move over here, move over there. Take three steps and turn left." I want to hear something about *why* I'm taking three steps. I want to hear something about motivation, like "You want to stalk the man," and then I'll just fly.

Now I did *Fiddler on the Roof* on the road. I never opened on Broadway because my character got cut the week before the opening in New York. But I got to watch Zero Mostel and Jerry Robbins work. They had a wonderful relationship in which Jerry would say, "It's not right, Zero." And Zero would change it. "That's not right." He'd change it. "That's not right." And Zero would change it every time and give him something completely different and that fast. Now I can't work that way. That's genius. Zero said to me later, "He really doesn't know what he's looking for, but when he sees it he knows what it is." So there's that kind of director and no less a genius than Elia Kazan who says, "You're doing this because . . ." and the operative word is *because.*

RH: The director for *Cat on a Hot Tin Roof*, Howard Davies, what sort of relationship did you have with him?

CD: I think he's probably one of the best directors I've ever worked with.

RH: Why?

CD: Because he's not only a director, he's a teacher. He's teaching you a fundamental way of working in which he makes you create the idea yourself. And what that means is that anything is possible. I would go anywhere and do anything to work with that man. And a nice man besides. If you have a suggestion, he'd say, well, let's try it. He didn't have the adamancy of some directors who think it's got to be *my* way or no way.

8

Charles Durning as Big Daddy in the 1990 revival of *Cat on a Hot Tin Roof*, Eugene O'Neill Theatre. Photo by Michael Tighe.

I did a piece on American Playhouse by Christopher Hampton called *Tales from Hollywood* which Howard directed. He called me from England and said, would I do it and I said, "yes," and he said but you don't know anything about it, and I said, "If you're directing it, I want to do it. That's enough for me."

RH: What was a bad situation you had with a director? You don't have to say who it is. What I'm interested in is what you didn't like about it.

CD: Well, there've been several directors I've worked with who just didn't know what the play was about. There are some directors who give you line readings. That infuriates me. There are some directors who are result-oriented—they want the end of the play before you've really started your work on it. And that irritates me because they don't allow you to do the process. Okay, if I'm still floundering after several weeks, start telling me. But give me a chance to find it for myself first.

I don't appreciate a director who says, "Put one foot here. Put the other foot there." And I've worked with those directors who have corded off the stage into four sections, and you have to be at a certain section at a certain line. It's like playing chess. And you're thinking about that instead of what's going on between you and the other actors. In this situation, the actor's instinct and thought process are crippled. Now, giving a suggestion is completely different. If the actor has any imagination, with the right suggestion, he can just *go*.

RH: Now you mentioned earlier a word *delineate*.

CD: Well, there are many things I do to delineate a character. First, I ask, what part of himself does this man think with? his head, his heart, his groin? Of course, we all have all three, but one of them is usually predominant. And throughout life, we all have all the passions in us: love, hate, anger, joy, fear. We're diabolical, cynical, all of them. Now I go to the zoo and I watch animals to study specific traits: the lion has dignity. The tiger has ferocity. The fox is sly. The otter is sweet. The snake is silent. A bird is twittering, nervous. That's the main characteristic.

We all have all of those in us. But it's like making a *pousse-café*—you lay the layers of liquor on top of each other, and you get varying colors. And it's all the layers of your character you have to figure out, and *how* the colors show themselves. Is it anger, is it love, is it lust, what? But there are several at the forefront and the others lie dormant. And so, I try to figure out all these things in the character.

Now the interesting thing is how one of these (maybe one not so clearly seen) can take over in a character. A man can be loving and deceitful at the same time. He can be a coward and at the same time he can be strong. He can be weak and determined. On a given day we don't know which is going to be there first. And you have to know all of these things about your character. And this, of course, is all the backstory.

And then there's something I very seldom talk about. Within all of us we have a secret place filled with sulfuric acid and bile and the most horrible thoughts.

. . . with Julie Harris in the West Coast premiere of *On Golden Pond* at the Ahmanson, Los Angeles, 1980. Photo by Jay Thompson.

RH: Absolutely. It's in me.

CD: Sure. It's in all of us. And that's what you often have to call on, and it's hard to do. Because you don't want anybody to know about it. Nobody in the cast has to know about this and even the audience doesn't know about it. But you know. And it's hard: dredging up that pit, that reservoir of unclean thought, and often you are surprised by what you find.

RH: In what role have you most used that aspect of yourself?

CD: Mainly on stage: in *Sweet Bird of Youth* and *Cat on a Hot Tin Roof.* But I did use it in *True Confessions.* I played this silent killer who never seemed to do anything wrong. He loved his family, loved his child, could entertain in a most friendly way. But he could also be a party to sawing

11

a woman in half—literally—just to get rid of her. I did another thing called *The Man Who Broke a Thousand Chains* with Val Kilmer. I played the warden who had these dire thoughts and who loved to torture the prisoners. But the important thing about a man like that is that you have to find the humanity in the man: he hires his brother-in-law to keep the family from starving.

RH: Now how much are you affected by a costume you wear?

CD: I treat a costume just like a suit I may be wearing in everyday life. If you are of that period, the costume is what you'd wear every day. It's like wearing a tuxedo: you become a little more elegant yourself because of the restrictions it puts on you. If you put on the regality of a king with the robes and crown and all for the coronation, then that's restricting, too. Whatever you're wearing is ordinary. For instance, you may have Tiffany silver in your house. But because it's what you eat with every day, it's not something fancy, it's just eating utensils.

RH: Who's an actor or actress you've loved being on stage with?

CD: That's easy. Colleen Dewhurst, Julie Harris, Maureen Stapleton, Madeline Kahn.

RH: Interesting. Julie Harris mentioned you when I asked her this question.

CD: Oh, really?

RH: Was *On Golden Pond* with her a good experience?

CD: The best. You know, when you're on stage with someone who knows how to create magic—and Julie does—she can help you look like you create it. No matter what she says about me, she creates it and you just steal a little of it. And of course, you take the credit for it. But she makes the sun shine and she makes the clouds come.

The thing about Julie is that she commits. Often people get self-conscious about certain things they do on stage, and it's because there's no commitment. I did another production of *On Golden Pond* years later with a very much respected actress. She said the rag doll was too much

12

for her to handle, the Indian dance was too "corny." See, she was thinking not like the character or *as* the character, but as herself judging, and that's no good. She said, "I'm going to cut this and cut that," and I said to her, "You're cutting the heart right out of your character." And she said, "What do you mean?" And I knew then that she just didn't get it; she couldn't commit.

"Working with Anne Bancroft—how often do you get a chance to work with spun glass?"

RH: What was it like to be on stage with Colleen Dewhurst?

CD: Colleen was a force of nature. When she smiled, the world opened up for you. We made several films together, too, but you know, I used to stand in the wings and just watch her. I used to watch Mostel too, and George C. Scott. That's really where I learned most of my acting. They honor you simply by being on stage with you.

RH: What would you say—we'll change the subject slightly here—is the biggest difference between acting on stage and acting for the camera?

CD: That's hard. Laurence Olivier was asked once if he had to retain only one thing for acting on stage, what would it be? And he said, his arms. And if he had to retain one thing on screen, what would it be? And he said, his eyes. And you know, if you look at the great screen actors, they have the ability to change expression through the eyes. Look at that much-underestimated actor Gary Cooper. He could make you know exactly what he was thinking.

RH: What was a film experience you really liked?

CD: Well, I'd say working with Duval and DeNiro on *True Confessions* was pretty wonderful. We are old friends and because of our past together, we had a built-in relationship. You don't have to work at the relationship because it's already there. All kinds of problems can occur when you don't know the person. But that wasn't the case here. I understand now why they had those stock companies back in the early movies. You worked with the same people, and you knew them well and how they worked and what they would do. I knew exactly what these guys were going to do and how they were going to do it, so there were no unfortunate surprises. You can trust people in a situation like that.

RH: What was *To Be or Not to Be* like to work on?

CD: Working with Anne Bancroft—how often do you get a chance to work with spun glass? That woman is so anchored in her craft that she knows how far over she can go. She was as much, if not more, of a delight in that role as Carole Lombard in the original. And of course Mel Brooks is just naturally funny. When he directs you, that's even funny. When he shows you how it can be, you know you'll never be that good. You're just glad you had a shot at it.

RH: You were very fine in that. That was one of your Academy Award nominations, I believe. The other was for *The Best Little Whorehouse in Texas*.

CD: Well, I got that nomination because it came as a surprise to them that I could sing and dance.

RH: Now you're doing a very popular TV series, *Evening Shade*. What's that like?

CD: Well, look at the talent on that show: Burt Reynolds, Elizabeth Ashley, Marilu Henner, Hal Holbrook, Ossie Davis, Ann Wedgworth, Michael Jeter. So much talent.

RH: Now when you do the same character every week but in different situations, is there any difference in the way you approach that than the way you'd approach, say, a movie?

CD: Not really. The only difference is that the character is already delineated. I don't have to work on that aspect week by week. We already know what he is: he's a good doctor who just happens to have these quirky habits. And he's married to an absolutely batty woman whom he adores. And he's a little batty himself. But he's also concerned and loving.

14

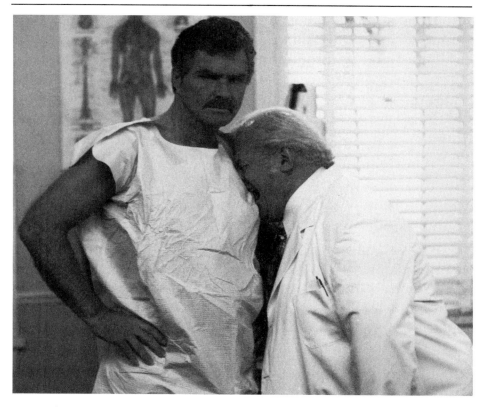

. . . with Burt Reynolds in the weekly television series *Evening Shade*, 1990. Photo © 1990 CBS Inc., courtesy of CBS Photography.

And he's got a good heart: his wife had a child many years before, and he never let her know that he knew about it because he loved her so much. He has a largeness of soul that's really bottomless, but he does make *faux pas*. So the character's already delineated and you just play the new specifics on each episode. The episode we did last night was with Ossie Davis and Ruby Dee and it's about Martin Luther King Day, and he keeps insulting Ruby Dee without meaning to—there's no real animosity behind it.

RH: What's the worst thing that ever happened to you on stage?

CD: There have been many "worst things" that happened to me on stage, but I'll tell you one. In *Cat on a Hot Tin Roof*, I'm in full view of

15

the audience through a whole act. I make my entrance and as soon as I sit down on the sofa, I realize my fly is open. So I'm sitting and I sort of move my hand over to cover it, and then I stand and walk behind the couch. Then I realize it's not stuck, it's torn. And I think, should I take the jacket off and try to cover it, and meanwhile, the guy is waiting for his cue, right? So I gave him his cue, but I never sat down again or faced forward through the whole act. I played it behind the birthday cake and behind Brick.

RH: Did they know what was going on?

CD: No, none of them knew. Now when the actor playing Brick came off, he said, "What the hell is going on?" And I said, "Look," and he said, "Holy shit!" Now Gerry Freedman the director was there seeing the show that night. And I asked him if he noticed anything peculiar in the second act with me, and he said, "No, it was great." And I said that my fly was open, and he said, "I thought you were playing pain."

RH: Is there anything you think we may have left out?

CD: There's an old trick I used to use. I haven't done it in years. When you are having trouble learning lines, write it down. Write the whole speech down. Or, if you just don't understand the speech, Shakespeare in particular, just say it in your own words. That way you might get some of the meaning of what's going on. Then you have to say the line, but the meaning as you've figured it out is with you. And you understand the thoughts behind it.

RH: As you look back at your career, what do you think of?

CD: You know, if I were an acting teacher, and I'm not—I don't know how to teach acting—I would have young actors learn ballroom dancing as opposed to tap or modern or ballet, because that's all solo. In ballroom, you have to consider the other person. I'd have men dance with women and with men, and vice versa. I'd have men lead, and I'd have women lead. And the purpose would be to get used to depending on someone else. Many actors act alone because they don't know how to interact.

16

You know, I'm learning all the time. Somebody asked Ralph Richardson what acting was all about, and he said—and he was eighty-three at the time—"I don't know. I'm just beginning to get the hang of it." You think you've got something solved, but it never comes up again in just the same way, even when you do the same play again. Because you've got a different actor over here saying, what about this? People tell me I'm there, but I sure as hell don't feel it. I'm still trying to get the hang of it.

Photo by Bill Crockett.

That Wonderful Strange Alchemy

JULIE HARRIS

This interview took place on Monday, March 23, 1992, in the living room of Miss Harris's midtown Manhattan hotel suite. She was in the second week of rehearsals for the role of Lettice Douffet in the national tour of Peter Shaffer's *Lettice and Lovage*, a role she described as "overwhelming." A few days before she had apologized to me on the phone for being able to give "only an hour" for this interview. "Every moment with this role," she explained, "is precious to me." I would gladly have accepted fifteen minutes because Julie Harris has represented for me the highest standards of acting for more than thirty years. My beginning knowledge of what acting was stemmed from having seen her in the film version of *The Member of the Wedding* when I was a child. Her performance as the motherless, twelve-year-old tomboy Frankie Addams was so convincing that I thought Frankie was a boy. It took my mother several hours to convince me that Julie Harris was not only a girl, but a woman. All of her performances are indelible in this way, and that's why she has had a five-decade career, which is still flourishing.

Roy Harris: When you read a script and say to yourself, 'I've got to do this,' what makes you feel that?

Julie Harris: Well, if the part touches something in me. For instance, the producers of Paul Zindel's *And Miss Reardon Drinks a Little* wanted me to play Catherine, and I read the play and my heart went out to Anna. Because Anna, to me, had the heartbeat of the play. She was the one who had had the nervous breakdown. Her crisis was the most immediate. She was the most vulnerable. Not every part has to be vulnerable, but it has to have—oh, I suppose you can call it—a moment of glory. By that I mean something that changes you as you listen to it. There was a speech about the woman upstairs (who is the school supervisor) and Anna is temporarily out of the school because of this breakdown. The teachers get together and buy her a present. And the present is a gold cross. And Anna says, no, I don't wear crosses. And the speech she has after that is just beautiful writing.

RH: Once you've decided to do a role, how much preparation do you do before you go into rehearsal?

JH: Well, that depends. I'm rehearsing a play right now by Peter Shaffer, *Lettice and Lovage*, and it's a very long part. Do you know it?

RH: Yes, very long. But a fascinating character for you.

JH: It's a very complex part with an extraordinary way of speaking. It's not realistic, her way of speaking; it's almost archaic. Fortunately for me I've had many months to study it. I've been able to learn it before rehearsal. So in rehearsal I'm not bound by struggling for what word is next. You can just sing it out, which this part needs: a boldness. Once you've got the words, the rhythm of the woman is inside you.

Now, of course, if it's a part about a character who actually lived, like *The Lark*, then there's all that research. Reading all that history about St. Joan is really quite fascinating, and it gives you the facts. Then your imagination works.

RH: I imagine when you did *The Belle of Amherst*, you had a great time doing research on Emily Dickinson.

JH: Yes, but of course before I began working on the *Belle*, I'd been reading about her, let's see, it must have been about sixteen years. I had done several records of her poems for Caedmon. But I went to her house. I've always believed that that's the extraordinary thing about playing a real person. If you're able, go to their childhood house. You can look through the window. In doing research on Emily Dickinson, I went through every room. I walked where she walked. When I worked on

Julie Harris as Lettice Douffet in Peter Shaffer's *Lettice and Lovage*, National Tour, 1992. Photo by Martha Swope.

Isak Dinesen, I went to her home in Africa, and it was fascinating. It does something to you to see what they saw. You can see in your mind's eye what they saw. It's a certain kind of attachment to the character that you can't get another way.

RH: In *Lucifer's Child*, through what you saw you created the people that we didn't see. For instance, when you have the memory of the mother.

JH: Oh, yes, that.

RH: And the memory of the father. And particularly when you describe yourself dancing with Marilyn Monroe. You made them so vivid, those memories, that they were alive for us. That must have to do with the research, too.

JH: I don't know where the connection comes from. That's very mysterious, you know. It's what makes you love some person and just like some other person. And I don't know why that is. It's some wonderful strange alchemy.

RH: When you're working in rehearsal, is there any particular preparation you do the night before?

JH: Something specific? Well, I don't think so, no. Because in the first week of rehearsal, I try to be very open. I never read the playwright's stage directions. Isn't that awful? I don't know if it's lazy or if I expect it to fall into place. *She picks up the cat here.* Well, I never pay any attention to that because I think we'll find where to pick up the cat. I try not to figure things out too quickly beforehand.

RH: In rehearsal what do you most want from other actors? What are you looking for from them in the process?

JH: I take whatever is there. And everybody works differently. Roberta Maxwell, who's doing this *Lettice and Lovage* with me, is meticulous. It seems to me that she doesn't force anything. She doesn't come flamboyantly with anything too quickly. She's almost like a blank slate for the first week, soaking things up. It's wonderful for me. As Lettice I have to take her persona even as she seems to be wool-gathering.

RH: Has there been an actor (or perhaps several) with whom you felt you had an unusually good relation on stage?

JH: Oh there are quite a lot. Boris Karloff was absolutely amazing in *The Lark*. Estelle Parsons, too, but that was sort of mixed because she can be very difficult. But she was so wonderful on stage. And, of course, Charlie Durning was always a blessing to be on stage with.

RH: What made it so special with him?

JH: It was just a complete giving. With Charlie in *On Golden Pond*, I believed that what we were doing was happening right then. We weren't

22

. . . . as Emily Dickinson in William Luce's *The Belle of Amherst*, 1977. Photo courtesy Billy Rose Collection, New York Public Library at Lincoln Center.

acting. We were truly like two people just living out their lives, perhaps in a heightened reality.

RH: Have you worked with someone with whom the experience was very difficult?

JH: Well, Rex Harrison was mighty difficult but he was so wonderful that you overlooked it. It was amazing to be with him on stage. Ethel Waters, on the other hand, was an angel. I can safely say she was the greatest actress I've ever worked with on stage. We had a wonderful time on *The Member of the Wedding*.

RH: What made it so great?

JH: She was so instinctive. Now she wouldn't talk about any method with you. She just did it. She lived it, you know. You could feel that she was thinking, "I don't have to think about pain. It's here." She was wonderful to work with. I was so inexperienced and she was very patient. She and Brandon and I just had a wonderful time being together on stage. She was very nervous about learning the lines, I think. And she used to say, "This isn't the way I would talk." And Harold Clurman, who was directing it, would say, "Just say it the way you want." And she'd paraphrase. But she would always come back to Carson's words.

RH: You mention *instinctive*. Would you say that you are an instinctive actress or one more given to plan?

JH: Well, I suppose I have a plan. You know it's different from play to play actually. When I'm doing a real story, a woman who really lived, I don't have to plan anything because my reaction from the beginning was so strong. With a fictional person though, I guess my approach is different: then I have to try to particularize. It takes me longer and I'm much more unsure of myself. If I'm going to do a real person I have a built-in empathy, so I don't know if I have a strong plan there.

One of the great thrills for me was working with someone like Ethel Waters, who was so instinctive. You know, Geraldine Page was an idol of mine. I think as actresses, we are very different. But I would easily lay down my life for Gerry Page. I just adored her. She was overwhelmingly real. And poetic. Around her, watching her, I always felt like I had two left feet.

RH: One of the reasons I got interested in how actors work and finding out more about it was watching Joan Allen and Peter Friedman work in rehearsal in *The Heidi Chronicles*. Joan is so instinctive and Peter is a master of good plan, and yet the two techniques in the final product were wonderful.

JH: I guess I have a plan but I do find myself changing a lot of what I do. During the first week, I throw myself around, go here and go there,

. . . with Ethel Waters and Brandon de Wilde in the 1952 film version of Carson McCullers' *The Member of the Wedding*. Photo courtesy of Columbia Pictures.

and then at the end of that week, I find myself saying, 'Why on earth did you do that, Julie? Don't go there. Go there.' I also usually think, 'I should never have attempted this role. It's too much.' Then I sort of hang on by my fingernails and my teeth. Then slowly, slowly something begins to happen.

RH: Have you ever felt you've done a role and just didn't get it?

JH: Well, you know I never felt I got any role completely—ever.

RH: I imagine that most good actors feel that way.

JH: I'd always like to do it over. The fortunate thing about a one-woman show is that you can come back to it. Often you do. On *The Belle of Amherst*, I worked with Charles Nelson Reilly, and we did it and it was a success. And I did it several times more. Once, I did it after having not done it for many months, for a benefit in California at my church. I suddenly realized that I should be doing the opening in a certain way. The audience must feel almost as if you are not going to

25

be able to do it. That Emily's so frightened she can't speak. And in that moment when I walked out with the teacart, I began to think, 'This was a mistake. I shouldn't have done this.' I was so frightened I wanted to leave the stage. I almost broke out into a sweat. I sat down and said, "It's not easy for me to talk to you." And it all seemed to fall into place for me, and this was much later. A friend who had seen it earlier in New York said to me afterwards, "Oh Julie, I didn't know what was going to happen, whether you were going to keep going or not." In acting it's got to have that wonderful do-or-die.

I had a wonderful movement teacher. He was Italian. He taught at the Shakespeare Festival in Canada. In class, he had us be lifted up. He had me put my foot on someone's knee and then the person would lift me very quickly up onto his shoulders. It was frightening. You'd get the feeling, 'No, no. The risk is too great. Stop.' And as an actor you have to convey that. Am I going to sink or swim? It makes for that feeling of emergency that's so necessary.

RH: What's the chief difference, for you, between doing a one-woman show and doing a show with other actors (other than, of course, the obvious difference: you're by yourself)?

JH: It's a different concentration I think. When you're all by yourself, you control everything. With other actors, everyone controls; you can drop the ball occasionally, and know that someone else will pick it up (at least you hope they will; if they don't, you've got a mess). When other actors are there, it's a great source of comfort.

RH: What are you looking for from a director?

JH: Well, a concept I think that you as an actor can see and relate to and try to reach for. This would mean that he'd present qualities in the play that you haven't seen there.

RH: Do you have a favorite director, or one you particularly relate to?

JH: I love Charles Nelson Reilly. Harold Clurman. Elia Kazan, of course. John Van Druten was a wonderful director. He enjoyed actors so much. Thinking of him now makes me laugh. He felt actors were a little like

26

poodles in the circus—that we need a lot of reassurance and tender loving care. He was very good at saying, "You can do it. You can do it," and knowing how to have us do it. He could also be stern and not let you get away with anything.

Acting is a discipline, you know. There's so much inside your heart, inside your head. And you can't do that yourself. The director's eye is so important. Someone you trust.

This part in *Lettice and Lovage*—I've never done anything like this. It's so bold. There's not a moment when she feels sorry for herself. She's a very brave woman and she comes from a very brave mother. And I'm trying to find those qualities in myself. It's not easy.

"You know, Geraldine Page was an idol of mine. I think as actresses, we are very different. But I would easily lay down my life for Gerry Page. I just adored her. She was overwhelmingly real. And poetic."

RH: This is one of the reasons I respect actors. You're brave. You have to go out there every night, and it completely depends on you. No matter how great the set, the costumes, lights—unless you're making it happen, it's no good. It's why as a stage manager I believe that you do everything you can to have actors happy in their situation.

JH: And you know that's why when actors are in a really unhappy situation, they fight like anything to get happy. When I was getting ready to open in *A Shot in the Dark*, the producers told me a terrible story about Annie Girardot who had a great success with the play in Paris. The night before opening her producers came to her and told her she was awful. I don't know why they would do that. But she had to go on on opening night fighting what she had been told. Actually it sort of fuelled her. Instead of sinking, she got above it. That story has always stuck with me.

RH: Now, in your career, you did one musical.

JH: Oh, yes, *Skyscraper*. You remember that?

RH: It was the first Broadway musical I ever saw. I think I was still in high school. Of course, I bought the album. I listened to it recently. I can hum the first song you sang. [*hums*] "What's so abnormal about imagination?"

JH: [*sings quietly*] "What's so peculiar about preoccupation? What's so eccentric about and makes it such a crime if I'm a person who runs away from troubles and hassles, preferring to spend the day in Spanish castles? What makes a dreary world seem bright? An occasional flight of fancy?"

RH: Is there any difference in your approach to a musical role than the way you'd approach any other?

JH: Well, I took singing lessons every day right through the end of the run. I'm not a trained singer, so I had to. In previews, I got a cold and missed two performances. But once we were open, I didn't miss a single performance in ten months. Sometimes at the end of the week, I can tell you, my voice was hoarse and very tired. As a singer I didn't know what I was doing, and I was terrified. They all said to me, Oh wait till you hear the overture every night. And it does do something to you that doesn't happen any other way. Even if it's not the greatest score, the music itself electrifies you, gives you something you can't get any other way. But it was a terrifying experience, not unlike when I did Juliet.

RH: Why was Juliet so terrifying?

JH: First, because it's a great part, and really when I did it, I didn't have the classical training. I had played the third witch in a production of *Macbeth* when I was nineteen. Playing Juliet was like climbing a mountain every night, and you keep falling down and your knees get bloody and you fall again. And then you pick yourself up, bloody, but you keep going. But what a part!

RH: It's interesting that you say this about Juliet. When I interviewed Bobby Leonard he had just done Romeo, and he said it was the hardest

28

. . . in the Broadway musical *Skyscraper*, 1965. Photo courtesy Bettmann Archive.

part he'd ever played. He felt he wouldn't understand it until he was fifty, if then, and then he'd be too old to play it.

JH: Well I'm not sure I could do Juliet justice even now. That's how monumental it is. Juliet is a huge part, with all the emotions, "My bounty is as boundless as the sea, my love as deep, for both are infinite." That's a huge emotion for anyone, let alone a fourteen-year-old. And the transitions are so swift. I wasn't prepared for them.

RH: What's the biggest difference as you see it between creating a character for the stage and creating one for film?

JH: I always say that you want it to be the truth wherever it is. But the technique at arriving at that truth is always different. In film it's just very tedious work. You do it over and over and over again.

RH: In film do you have a favorite role, or a role that you were basically pleased with?

JH: Well, I liked my work in *Reflections in a Golden Eye*.

RH: Oh, yes. Allison. The one who knits. Why do you like that one?

JH: Well, probably because I fought so hard to get it. John Huston didn't want me.

RH: And why not?

JH: Well, he wanted Margaret Leighton. And when it came time she was doing something else and wasn't available. He tried everybody but me, but I kept pursuing it through my agent. I even did a screen test for it. I felt I had a very personal attachment to that character, partly through Carson, I think. And when I see it now I think, 'Oh, yes, well you did what you wanted to.' She was very fragile looking and rather strange, and I fought for all that. There was a particular way I saw her, and I fought for it all to get on screen.

RH: *The Member of the Wedding* is a favorite of mine. Were you pleased with your work there?

JH: No.

RH: It's wonderful work. Why not?

JH: I think precisely because I'd done it on the stage; it's a different thing in film, a different performance. I never felt I got the rhythm right.

RH: Do you think it's because it felt so different? Because, you know, it's a grand performance.

30

JH: I just never felt comfortable.

RH: Well, no discomfort registers when you see it on the screen. You know, you've had an amazing four-and-a-half decade career. You've created some pretty memorable women: Frankie, or course. Abra in *East of Eden*, Joan in *The Lark*.

JH: Mrs. Lincoln. Don't forget Mrs. Lincoln.

RH: No. The drug addict singer Betty Fraley in *Harper*. Miss Thing in *You're a Big Boy Now*.

JH: I've been very lucky. For Hallmark I did *Johnny Belinda*, *Victoria Regina*, *Little Moon of Alban*, *Anastasia*, and *Florence Nightingale*.

RH: Do you have a favorite role?

JH: Well, I don't think so. I love Emily Dickinson. Always I want to go back to doing that. And then Isak Dinesen is close to my heart. I also did a play about Dora Carrington and Lytton Stratchey called *Under the Ilex* by Clyde Talmadge. And then I did a play about Mrs. Tolstoy by Donald Freed—*The Countess*. Now that's a story, let me tell you. She'd be nursing a child and then copying all her husband's work of the day on *War and Peace*.

RH: Let me ask you this: Do you think there's a true place for critics in theatre. And if so, what is it?

JH: You know, I think everyone—a painter, writer, musician, actors even—everyone wants his work seen, appraised. Now I saw *Sight Unseen* Sunday afternoon, and I went because Mr. Rich's review made me very excited. Also, his wonderful review of *Marvin's Room*. It's a wonderful play. The two sisters, and those boys: the one with the soulful eyes who reads and the angry one, he's so fine. You see, the good review has a lot of power, and the theatre needs that help. So the critics certainly have a place. But I was hurt, for instance, when Mr. Rich reviewed *The Visit* recently, and he said it had no "star power." Well, that's cruel. And as Tennessee says, "I cannot accept deliberate cruelty."

RH: Have you ever felt, at any time, that a critic saw something about your work and that it was understood?

31

JH: Yes. For instance, when we opened *And Miss Reardon Drinks a Little* in Boston, Kevin Kelly wrote this review. It was amazing, not just because he liked it, but he understood it. His review was like he dreamed the play.

And then I had a similar experience years ago when I did June Havoc's play, *Marathon '33*, a show I liked enormously. There's a scene where Lee Allen and I are dancing, struggling to keep up on our feet. It's just the two of us struggling to keep on our feet. Joe Don Baker is the emcee and Conrad Janis and his Tail Gate 5 did the music. And it's six in the morning, a musician comes in, sits down at the piano, and starts playing *Say It Isn't So*. And there was this one shaft of light—from Tharon Musser—and it was like seeing Christ. The light was like Tintoretto. This essense of light. And *The Christian Science Monitor* wrote about this light with that kind of significance. Kids during the depression would buy a ticket to watch people do these horrible, long marathon dances. It would be equivalent to our taking homeless people today and putting them on the stage and people paying to see them.

RH: Have you ever felt that something you were trying to do just wasn't seen at all?

JH: Well, no, because perhaps I've been lucky, but someone along the way has always caught it. Maybe it wasn't an official critic but someone. For instance, our interpretation of Emily Dickinson wasn't always liked, but many did like it, and that helped.

RH: You've played many roles but there must have been some you haven't played. If you could play any role ever written, what would it be?

JH: Nina in *The Seagull*. I'm too old, of course, but that's one I never got to do when I could have. There's a woman in Chatham where I live who runs a theatre company. And she was doing a benefit and asked me to do a reading. She wanted Shakespeare I think, but I chose Nina. So I did get to do that last scene of Nina.

RH: If you could work with any actor, who would it be?

JH: Well, I never worked with Marlon Brando or Marilyn Monroe. I'd like to work with Woody Allen. And Michael Gambon.

RH: Well, I've used up my hour. Should we stop?

JH: I think so. Lettice is calling me.

RH: With your career, you know, we could talk an hour every day for a month—and still not do justice to it.

JH: Perhaps you're right. It has seemed to endure.

Photo by David Spagnolo.

Between Two People

RON RIFKIN

This interview took place on Wednesday, June 26, 1991, in the Studio Theatre at Playwrights Horizons in New York City. It was four days before Jon Robin Baitz' *The Substance of Fire*, in which Ron Rifkin was playing the role of Isaac Geldhart, closed its initial New York run. (Six months later, it reopened and ran for seven months at Lincoln Center Theater, and later had quite a successful run at the Mark Taper Forum in Los Angeles.) A large part of the interview is about the development of this performance, which was described by one New York critic as "career transforming," and which won all the off-Broadway best actor awards that season. The role of Isaac was written especially for Ron and was the beginning of the playwright/ actor association of Robbie Baitz and Ron Rifkin.

Roy Harris: When you first read a script and say, "I have to do this role," what makes you want to do it?

Ron Rifkin: That's a good question. I think some kind of visceral connection happens; you identify with something. 'I know this person. I know these people I would like to be a part of.' Or, 'I'm afraid of this person,' or 'I don't like this person.' It's something that happens instantly, viscerally, that makes you feel that this experience is going to be exciting, or scary, or dangerous, or beautiful, or all of those adjectives.

RH: Once you get the role, what sort of work do you do before you actually begin the rehearsal process?

RR: It depends on the script.

RH: What do you mean? Take Isaac in *The Substance of Fire* for instance.

RR: That's an odd circumstance because Robbie wrote it first as a one-act. We did it at Naked Angels which is kind of like home. No critics were coming so I had nothing to worry about. Just exploration.

RH: But with Isaac, you knew you had to have an accent. Did it come easily for you? Did you think about it beforehand?

RR: Robbie gave me some guidelines with the accent. I knew the kind of sound he wanted. I also knew the person whose accent he liked. It was a kind of in-and-out accent, and I knew for the theatre an in-and-out accent would sound like I couldn't sustain an accent.

RH: Of course, that's what I'd think.

RR: Because he's such an incredible writer, Robbie throws in a lot of slang expressions, *kiddo* and *crapolla*, things like that, and that gave the impression of what he wanted without my having to lose the accent. You know, I grew up in a part of New York where there were so many Europeans that it was really sort of part of me already. I've done European accents before. This one was special because Isaac is such an educated man. I wanted his elegance to show through.

RH: You've done Isaac three times: the one-act version at Naked Angels; the first two-act version at Long Wharf, and now the Playwrights Horizons version. Did the accent change over the course of this year-and-a-half?

RR: They tell me it has. I can't really be a judge of that. They tell me this is the cleanest, most cultured, the most refined. Rob Morrow, who played Aaron in both the previous productions, said that this accent is the most elegant. But that may be because of the slight English accent I've given it.

RH: Take this role, or actually any role. Before you get to rehearsal, do you ever research?

RR: I think these are the guidelines for me: if I feel so unfamiliar with the profession or the nature of the work that this person does, then it behooves me to explore. If I feel that the lack of knowledge is going to

36

Ron Rifkin as Isaac Geldhart in Jon Robin Baitz' *The Substance of Fire*, Lincoln Center Theater, 1992. Photo by Martha Swope.

get in my way because I won't know the behavior of, say, a judge, I'll research. Once I was doing a movie, playing a defense attorney. There was a lot of legalese involved. A friend of mind is an attorney and I went with him to court and just watched.

Once I did a play in which I had to be in a wheelchair. Sally Kellerman was playing my wife. So we got the wheelchair and Sally pushed me around the streets. I wanted to get a sense of what people feel when they see a grown man in a wheelchair and what he feels being in it. So in that sense I guess I do research.

RH: Okay, let's say we've had the first day of rehearsal. We've read through the play, and tomorrow you're going to work on the first fifteen pages of the script in rehearsal. What kind of work, if any, do you do the night before?

RR: My process is the rehearsal process. I get off book as late as I can. I don't like to impose on myself a pattern of speech until I feel comfortable with who this person is. A lot of actors come in knowing the lines. I've worked with actors like that, and it can be a problem. To learn beforehand, well, I think it's dangerous, because you can set something on your own that precludes finding out what's happening between two people. The real substance is what's happening between two people at that moment, in that space.

RH: When you get into rehearsal, what are you looking for from other actors? What is an ideal situation with you and, say, two other actors?

RR: Well, first, one hopes for the kind of personality mix that allows all of us to feel as free as we need to feel so that all the creative instincts can be released. I hope that nobody will be judging me. I try not to judge others but it's hard for me because I'm a very judgmental person. Of course, I want to work with talented people.

RH: What do you like least about the way other actors can work?

RR: Well, I don't like it when other actors give me notes in rehearsal, and that's happened sometimes. Basically, I don't like assholes. The rehearsal work situation is like any work situation. I like people to treat me the way I hope to treat them: with respect.

You know, I did one play three times. I did it first in the small Taper space, and it was successful so they brought it back to the mainstage. Then it went to New York. I was the only one who did all three productions. I had three different wives, three different mothers, three different fathers. My experience with the play was very different with each production. There was one woman playing my wife, in the mainstage production, whom I couldn't bear. Every time she looked at me, I wanted to scream. She had some really bad habits and she was a substance abuser. She abused substances in rehearsals and during performances. She had a totally different way of working than me. And she hadn't done much

38

. . . with Patrick Breen, Jon Tenney, and Sarah Jessica Parker in *The Substance of Fire*, Playwrights Horizons, 1991. Photo by Peter Cunningham.

theatre. During rehearsals, I lost it a lot, even during some performances. Being stoned on stage makes me absolutely crazy. It was horrible. Because the relationship of ours in the play was of such a nature, our difficulty together worked for us in the play. I don't think anyone in the audience ever knew there was a problem.

Often what happens, it seems to me, is that as you get into rehearsal you become to each other, as human beings, what the character relationships are. You take on the characteristics of the people you are playing. So that if the nature of the relationship is combative, you often become that way in the process. If you are skilled enough, you know that's happening and you let it be.

RH: Well, it seems to me that's what happened with you and the three actors playing the Geldhart children in *Substance of Fire*. That warm-up in the dressing room . . .

RR: That banter back and forth among the four of us is very, well, very Geldhartian. It's interesting how that's worked out. In the rehearsal process, there was one actor, as you remember, who took up a lot of time. And that's all right, that's his need. I never thought that I would get to love him as much as I do. My performance towards him has changed since we opened. For instance, the place in the play where I touch his cheek.

RH: Yes, when you say about buying the Hitler postcard, "It wasn't cheap."

RR: Yes. You were aware of that?

RH: Sure. That's part of my job. I remember the first time it happened. I watched it closely for three performances to make sure I felt it was right, you know, since it was new.

RR: In both previous productions, I never touched Aaron. But my relationship with this actor is totally different: sort of aggression-affection. I think it's very right.

RH: Backing up a little. As you work on a character, do you ever get a mental picture of what he should look like?

RR: Yes, I do. And sometimes it will actually get in the way. For instance, sometimes the writer will say something. I try not to let it bother me, though. Because, quite frankly, if this play had been written independently of me—if Robbie had just written it, and I had auditioned, I would not have gotten it. I suspect it would have gone to someone who looked totally different from me. In their minds, people stereotype. They say, 'Oh, this character is sixtyish; he's tall; he's very European.' Well, I'm not European; I'm not sixtyish. I'm just me. But it was in me.

RH: How much are you affected, in rehearsal, by how you think a character should dress, or how he should look?

RR: Oh, enormously. That's why in rehearsal I'll wear a jacket, something I think he might wear. First of all, as a human being, I am enormously affected by clothes.

RH: Are shoes important to you?

RR: Yes, very much. It's how you touch the earth. It's how you meet it, and the way every character meets the earth is completely different.

RH: I hate to use this word because it's so overused, but I can't think of a better one: did you find Isaac's journey through the play in the actual rehearsal process?

"Communication is the hardest thing between director and actor. Actually, it's the hardest thing between people. Ultimately, it's all in the communication."

RR: Yes, but you know, I'm still finding it.

RH: I know that. I assume exploration of a certain kind is never over. Did you come to a point in rehearsal, or more likely in performances, where you felt, I think I've got it now. You're shaking your head.

RR: I'm shaking my head when you say, "I have it now." There are some times when I think I *may* have it. Never in rehearsal. Because you really can't tell what you have until you have an audience. You learn so much from them. Remember last Sunday's performance? It was a particularly enlightening one for me because no one laughed. Nothing. And you know as well as I do that there are very funny things in this play. I often feel if they're not laughing, they're not liking it. And I'm depressed afterwards. But this particular audience, well, it was beyond laughter for them. It was almost a holy experience. These were sophisticated people. And I learned that you can't make judgments about an audience. You don't know what's going on in their heads. You've just got to do it and keep learning. And I don't feel that I've learned everything about Isaac—hardly. I'm pretty close to Isaac. How many performances have we done here?

RH: As of tonight, 134.

RR: And I feel with Isaac there's still a lot to learn. Because I'm not Isaac, and I don't have children and I've never experienced what he has about them. But I like him so much.

RH: What is your strongest point of identification with him, simply as one human being to another? The thing, I suppose, that made you feel, "I can do this."

RR: Because he's so much like my father. It thrills me to play aspects of my father on stage. I've never done that, at least not consciously. And it also has allowed me to understand parts of him that I thought I'd never understand. It enabled me to experience parts of my father I'd never experienced.

RH: How much are you affected by what your friends say about the play or about your performance?

RR: You know, my ego is fragile, and so I want everybody to like it. But I really don't listen to much. I used to, however. The three I listen to the most are, for obvious reasons: Robbie, Dan, and Iva.

RH: Well, that makes sense. The playwright, the director, and the person you're closest to. We're sort of talking around this, but I'll ask it anyway: how much do you use specific things in your own life when you work on a character?

RR: Oh, always. I think, first, that you incorporate a lot of that unconsciously, and then when you're in trouble, you ask: when in my life have I been like this? what in my life makes this situation clearer, illuminates it? And with Isaac, it was very conscious in relation to my father.

RH: What are you looking for most from the director?

RR: That's a hard question because I've worked with so few good directors. But, the nature of my personality is such that I look for the director to be like God. And I'm almost always disappointed. I think the reason that Dan Sullivan is so brilliant is that he got the absolute best out of everyone. And he never bristled—well, once, when he was confronted with that actor who said something was stagey. But it was over quickly and never referred to again. When the director trusts that the actor has it all inside him, then he can do his best work, too.

. . . with Maria Tucci in *The Substance of Fire*, Lincoln Center Theater, 1992. Photo by Martha Swope.

I'll give you a good instance with Dan. There's the scene in the play, near the end, where Isaac talks about all the children and his wife. I had always done that angrily with a lot of ferocious hostility. Well, Dan said to me one night after an early preview, "You know, Ron, the audience really has to see Isaac fall apart, or there's no catharsis for them." In the previous productions it had never occurred to me that Isaac would fall apart. And I said, "Okay, but please don't push me." And he didn't. He trusted that it was in me, and it was.

RH: I know. I've watched Dan now with two different shows and two different companies with the same show. And he never pushes. He steers, and it's very subtle. He makes an actor feel as if it all came from them.

RR: I just finished working on a workshop piece with Jerome Robbins. Because he's a dancer, well primarily a choreographer, he will say to somebody, "This is what I want you to do. Put your left hand in this position, put your right hand in that position," and the dancer does it. So he would say to me as an actor, "I want you to do this." And I told him that I couldn't work that way. No actor can. I said, "If you say to me this emotion is red, well, red to you might mean this, and red to me might mean that. Your red could be my green. So you have to know that for me to do your red, you have to tell me that it's green." Communication is the hardest thing between director and actor. Actually, it's the hardest thing between people. Ultimately, it's all in the communication. You have to keep asking, what does this mean? what does it mean?

RH: What was the worst experience you've ever had with a director? You don't have to say who it is.

RR: This was on television. It was a director who ridiculed me. He was a very glib, very funny man. He wanted a particular thing and he wasn't getting it from me—this was about ten years ago, and I was a regular on this series. And the guy started to push me and push me and push me, and I started to cry. And I called him an asshole and told him he didn't deserve to be a director. And the other actor in the scene told him, "Don't you ever talk to an actor like that again." This was a director without any class whatsoever, and I mean class as a human being. I think that's what I'm most afraid of.

When you're working with people whose emotions are supposed to be readily available and who put themselves on the line all day, you have to treat them with respect, or you won't get the results you want.

RH: What do you see as the biggest difference between acting for the camera and acting on stage? And, do you prefer one to the other?

RR: Well, I guess I prefer acting on the stage. And probably because the roles I've gotten on stage are really more interesting than the ones I've done in film and television. The roles I get on stage are usually done in film by stars. That's just the way it works; that's the business of it.

Aside from that, my experience working in film is that (and some actors would disagree with me) you have to know your face and you have to know your body. That is not to say that you censor yourself. But onstage, if you laugh or cry or move a certain way, you don't have to worry about it. You just do it. But if you do the same thing in a film, the camera is close up. And if one's face has generous features (as mine does) it can become grotesque on film. Therefore, you have to know your body and your face and how they translate on film. You just don't worry that much on stage. Of course, if it's a period play, you have to know how to move in that particular time. But because it's so much more intimate and private on film, things have to be taken down, altered slightly. Sounds need to be changed.

For instance, if I were to do *The Substance of Fire* on film, the place where Isaac breaks down and cries, well, I'd need a lot of help from the director with how to do that. To cry on stage, there's distance; to cry on film, it's so intimate. So, it's not that you act any differently. It's just that you have to always be aware of the closeness. Not aware in the front of your mind, but in the back of it, and that awareness can't ever leave you. I'm not saying that you have to look pretty.

RH: No, I know what you mean.

RR: You hear film people say, "He's a stage actor." And you can do things on stage that you can't do on film. I could be looking at you like this, with me not seeming to do anything—I'm just looking—and the camera would pick up all kinds of things in the face. The camera can make it seem as if I'm thinking a thousand different things.

RH: What's the hardest thing about film acting?

RR: Keeping your concentration going. You know, shooting out of sequence isn't great, but it's not the real problem. In film, there is no beginning, middle, or end. There's no audience. There isn't that two-hour period where your adrenaline gets going and it doesn't stop until well after the curtain call. Also, you don't rehearse as much. That's a given.

RH: What is a typical day of shooting like?

RR: What happens is: I'm on the film set at 7:00 AM, which means I got up at 4:00. The director rehearses us for half an hour, and in this scene, let's say, I have a very long, emotional speech. We block it. The cinematographer is there. He watches the director. He tells the director, "I don't think this is going to work. We're not going to be able to light it." Then, you go off in the corner while they light it. That can take two to three hours. So now you do what's called the master shot: they shoot both of you together. And they do it many times. Then we shoot point-of-view shots. We shoot the other actor over my shoulder, and they shoot me over his shoulder. And each of those has to be lit. So you wait again. And there's anywhere from twenty minutes to an hour between each one of these. So by the time it's 4:00 o'clock, we finally get to my long emotional speech. And where is the energy? You have to have been conserving it. You have to learn to pace yourself; how to keep your energy with all the distractions around you. That's why some actors just don't socialize. I know someone who worked with Meryl Streep and said she's cold on the set. I don't think so. The woman was just saving herself. At the risk of people thinking she's cold, she was conserving her energy. And very wise she was.

RH: What was your worst moment on stage ever?

RR: When I wet my pants.

RH: Well, that's unique. Should I ask the details?

RR: Please don't. Also, once I was playing in *Take Me Along* and I came out on stage in the wrong costume. You know, there's an aspect of acting on stage that no one can understand unless they've done it, and that's breaking up on stage. When it happens it's so scary to me because all the stuff you're taught—you have an obligation, people have paid money, this is sacred—goes out the window. It's happened to everybody. When I start to go, it terrifies me. I looked at Maria the other night during the show and we both started to go and I thought, 'We can't do this. We're the only two here. There's no one to stop us.' All I could think was, if this happens, I'll laugh for the next twenty minutes. And I just dropped it.

RH: If you could play any role ever written, what would it be, who would direct it, and who would play opposite you? In other words, the ideal situation.

RR: Well, I'm not one of those actors who's always wanted to play Hamlet or Lear. I guess I would like to play Vanya and have Dan Sullivan direct it. That is some role. I think that would be pretty exciting.

46

RH: Do you think you are more an instinctive actor or more planned?

RR: Instinctive.

RH: I ask that question because part of my desire to do this book came from seeing two actors work together whose way of working was so different. One instinctive, one rather remarkably planned. But the end product was brilliant.

RR: Well it's interesting because you know it doesn't always work that way. I did a production of *The Three Sisters* where I played Andrei and Tyne Daly was Natasha. There was an actor playing Tuzenbach who I thought was so wonderful during rehearsals. He had studied with John Houseman. He had a beautiful voice and great diction. He was playing it so brilliantly; his technique was amazing. Then it came the night the critics were there. There was a scene of his just before I wheel the baby on in his carriage and I say, "What have I done with all the years?" It had been worked out so carefully so that I wheeled the baby on at a certain point. He was doing his love scene with Irina. And I watched him change everything he had done in rehearsal. It ruined not only my scene but also his own. It was abominably selfish. I was overwhelmed by the selfishness of it. That's the kind of actor I can't stand. You're out there only for yourself with no regard for the rest of the play. Awful. Just awful. Suddenly he was using his voice, his diction—everything he could use—to get the audience's attention. I find that sometimes with actors who have had a certain kind of training. When the training shows, it's sad. I would rather see a raw performance with real emotional energy than one of those diction performances.

Photo by Martin Christoper.

In Constant Struggle

S. EPATHA
MERKERSON

This interview took place on Friday, January 22, 1993, in a rehearsal room at Lincoln Center Theater. I had worked with Epatha as one of the stage managers of the Young Playwrights Festival 1991. I had watched her develop, and in only a month of performances, enrich the character of Mrs. Fletcher, a woman who had bludgeoned her retarded son to death, in David Rodriguez' one-act play *I'm Not Stupid*. Epatha brought to this somewhat sensational story a rather startling modesty, and she made you feel for this woman even as you had to hate her. I never forgot the performance, nor the amazing complexity of feelings it caused in me each night. It is one of the reasons I asked her to do an interview.

Roy Harris: When you read a script and say to yourself, "I've got to do this role," what makes you feel that?

S. Epatha Merkerson: Usually it's the struggle that the character has to go through. More than anything else the conflict of the person, I think, is what excites me.

RH: When you did *The Piano Lesson* was it Berniece's struggle that interested you?

SEM: Well, there was a combination of things with *The Piano Lesson*. First, it was the fact that August Wilson had written it, so I knew that whatever the character was, there would be something interesting about her. It was also the fact that Lloyd Richards was directing. I joined the cast after they had already played two different cities.

RH: I don't think I knew that.

SEM: I didn't originate it. Starletta Dupois did. For me it was the package. I knew the whole experience would be fulfilling.

RH: And was it an experience you remember with pleasure?

SEM: Absolutely. To be with a project, developing it for two years—a new play by August Wilson! I was a part of all the changes that we made on the road. I think that every aspiring actor—young actor, I mean—knows the ultimate is Broadway. And I always said I wanted to make it to Broadway before I turned forty . . . and I did. The whole process was a wonderful challenge.

RH: Do you prefer a new play over Shakespeare or Wilde?

SEM: I do. I really do because there hasn't been any standard set. There hasn't been any particular way of seeing the character. No one has a preconceived notion of who and what this is.

RH: Was it difficult taking over a role?

SEM: Lots of times when you replace someone, there's a problem with what the cast is locked into. If you're a weak person, you end up doing exactly what the first actor did. If you're a strong person, you end up really frustrated (because you see things differently) and it's locked into a pattern. What was rewarding for me in *Piano Lesson* was that I was allowed to participate as a creative entity.

RH: I just went through a similar experience on *The Sisters Rosensweig*. Frances McDormand (who was playing Pfeni, the youngest sister) left and Christine Estabrook took her place. Dan Sullivan the director wasn't able to be here so I had to put her in. And I had to deal with just what you were describing: Chris Estabrook is very strong, she had her own notions (as she should), and she happens to be very fine in the role. But I had to deal with Chris's need to explore her way of seeing Pfeni and

S. Epatha Merkerson with Rocky Carroll in August Wilson's *The Piano Lesson*, Walter Kerr Theatre, 1990. Photo by Gerry Goodstein.

then the fact that John Vickery, Jane Alexander, Madeline Kahn, and the rest of the cast had a package that already worked for them. They had to bend and then Chris had to yield sometimes. It was fascinating. Meanwhile, I was trying to maintain the integrity of what Wendy and Dan had created.

SEM: Those times when a person is coming into a show and everyone is willing to accept the particular view of a character are rare.

RH: Very rare.

SEM: And as a stage manager, well, you know. There have been times where I've been put into shows where you absolutely cannot get the

51

other actors to budge from what they're doing. And I think it's an insecure actor who won't accept a new entity. The secure ones have a feeling, 'Yeah, let's see what we can do differently.'

RH: When you first got Berniece,what sort of work did you do before you got to rehearsal?

SEM: None.

RH: Why not?

SEM: The only thing I did was read the script. Because, again, I'm coming into a situation that has already been set up, and before I do anything, I want to know how much I *can* do.

RH: Of course.

SEM: Certainly, though, as I read it, I had ideas and thoughts about who she was and her relationship to the people around her—and how she functions in the situations. But I didn't want to marry myself to anything because I was unsure what the situation was going to be: how much freedom to create would I have?

RH: Let's say you're doing another new play, and you're going to do it from the ground up. You get the script and you've got three weeks before you start, do you do any work before rehearsals start?

SEM: Again, basically, it's reading. Because I believe that theatre is collaborative. There's the writer, the director who has a concept, and there are other actors who have done (hopefully) what you've done: that is, read the script and come in with a certain sense of who the person is, how they relate to the other characters . . .

How you'll carry it out depends almost completely on what happens in rehearsal. When I read a play, I hear all the characters speaking the parts. Now when we sit down together at the table, something that I've read one way, the actor may see another way, and it changes my notion. So I really try to go in with some background information on the character and maybe a history of the person. And those are things that I might write out beforehand. It's mostly thoughts about where this

52

person was prior to the play and maybe some family life, something about a job.

RH: Do you create a whole history for a character?

SEM: Not always. It depends on the character. For instance, in *The Piano Lesson*, there was a great deal you found out about Berniece from what August had written. So what I did was try to find the history of Berniece and Boy Willie, what they were like as kids. Those are the things that I think would inform me in the rehearsal process. So I go into rehearsal with my perceptions of Boy Willie, and I don't ever express them to him. But my perceptions inform how I respond to everything he says and does.

"With a new play, you really watch how it happens. You know, it's all written down and then the minute the actors get up and start talking and moving, it has a whole different feel to it."

RH: Sometimes, does your history change because of something that happens in rehearsal?

SEM: Oh, yeah. Those times are interesting because if it's something that I've specifically written down, then it's kind of hard for me to relinquish. But, if they come in with something so good that I just can't fight, then, yeah, it will change. And I think that, too, is part of the excitement of doing a new play: those things that change your mind.

With a new play, you really watch *how* it happens. You know, it's all written down and then the minute the actors get up and start talking and moving, it has a whole different feel to it. To be a part of this process is the excitement, and it's why I tend to want to stay with theatre as much as I can.

RH: Do you ever do any kind of formal research?

SEM: Again it would depend on the character. Maybe the formal research would be finding out where they're from, what the climate was like, the outward circumstances. But if I think I can do it without formal research, then I won't. It's more spontaneous that way.

RH: If you play a person who is (or was) real, like Billie Holiday in *Lady Day at Emerson's Bar and Grill*, did you do any research there?

SEM: Absolutely. I got documentaries on Billie, I read her autobiography. I talked with musicians who had worked with her. That was, however, an unusual situation because I went in as a standby. Lonette McKee, who was playing it, was ill at the time, and I went on for the first time under duress. I had to learn the show very quickly, so my research came after I had actually done it. I got the script and eight days later I was doing it. Because I know my history, there were things I already knew about Billie that helped me. Once I got over that first performance and Lonette returned, I was able to take time and define things. And it turns out, when I took over the role full-time, the information continued. I even met Jimmy Monroe, who was her husband and who people claim started her on drugs. So when people came to the show, there were all these stories about her, and also from the musicians in the band. So there was definite research there.

RH: Now since it was a one-woman show, when you went on were you able to do *your* performance?

SEM: Well, again, this was a weird situation. I didn't agree with the way a lot of the show was directed. I think you can glorify the life of Billie's music and what it meant to our country's history and to music itself. But I don't think you can glorify a death from drugs.

So I had my own interpretation with the blocking that was given by the stage manager. And because I hadn't seen it (Lonette was ill when I was hired), there were a lot of things in the blocking I didn't understand, so I chose (within the boundaries) to do some things differently. And let me tell you, there was some resistance.

When the director came to see a gypsy run-through of my work that week, we had a big disagreement. Here was a white man, Belgian, and

54

. . . . as Billie Holiday in the Vineyard Theatre production of *Lady Day at Emerson's Bar and Grill*, Westside Arts Theatre, 1986. Photo by Carol Rosegg/Martha Swope Associates.

he was going to tell me about black women in the '50s. It was difficult at the beginning. But, because the very next day I was doing the show, they had to let me do what I knew and what I understood. I'm not saying I know better than directors—I hope it doesn't sound that way—but, in this case, I had to go on my own instinct.

Now when he saw the show, he understood where I was coming from. And at that point, I was allowed to find it. The one thing I was not able to do (because I didn't originate the part) was ask for cuts. There was a lot of extraneous stuff in the script.

RH: You know what I remember about it, among other things, of course, was the costume you wore. It looked like Billie had worn that dress too many times. It seemed to suffer the way Billie had; it was a symbol of her pained soul.

SEM: I guess in a way that dress worked but it really looked that way because the producers were too cheap to spend the money.

RH: I'm disappointed. I thought it was a brilliant design choice.

SEM: No, just penny-pinching producers. Well, I'm glad it worked for you.

RH: Let's back up a little. When you go into rehearsal and it's the third day on, say, *The Piano Lesson*, and you're going to work on Act I, scene 3. Do you do any sort of work the night before, any homework?

SEM: Definitely. If it's early in rehearsal, I just try to figure out what's going on in the scene: What's she after; where she's involved and how, or is she removed? what activity is going on? what part of the house we are in. What has gone on before that will bring us up to what will go on after. I tend to wait to learn lines because I want to know what everybody is doing. Once I sit down to learn the lines, that will come quickly because of the time I've spent in rehearsal. Certainly, I look the scene over with a fine-tooth comb to see what's going on here.

RH: When you're in rehearsal what are you looking for from other actors?

SEM: I just want the other actors to be as open as I hope I am. And I don't think I ask for any more than that. I would also like—if something's been set—for them to continue to do it. Although I am open to spontaneity. If you want to try something very different, just say, "Epatha, you know, I've been thinking of some things so if I do something a little weird, you know, stay with me."

RH: In rehearsal do you tend to be more spontaneous, or do you work more from a plan?

SEM: Spontaneous.

56

RH: That's what I'd have guessed.

SEM: Spontaneity allowed me to do *Piano Lesson* for two years. As we grew with the characters there would be these days where something would happen on stage, and at first you'd go, 'Whoa! What's this?' and then you'd say, 'Okay, I can take that.' See, you knew the actor had just discovered something.

RH: So I take it *Piano Lesson* was a good rehearsal situation for you?

SEM: Absolutely. Again, it was a quick one. It was also strange because I never auditioned for it. I had never met Lloyd Richards. I didn't know August Wilson. The casting director, Meg Simon, got me that job. And I will love her forever for it. But the rehearsal situation turned out to be most wonderful.

RH: How long did you rehearse before you actually played it?

SEM: Eight days.

RH: Jeez. Again!

SEM: Yeah, eight days, and then we were in Chicago doing it. It seems like eight days is the number for me.

RH: Maybe it's magic. Does there ever come a time in rehearsal when you think, "Well, I've got it," or at least, "I've got that moment"?

SEM: Oh, yeah. That's a wonderful time.

RH: When does it happen for you, or does it vary?

SEM: Well, you know, with *Piano Lesson*, it had to do with Epatha and with Berniece. At one point I had to play the piano, and I don't play. And Epatha was afraid of it, and Epatha stopped Berniece from playing. And then one day in rehearsal we got to the piano, and I was absolutely where I felt I needed to be, and I sat down and I played, and Berniece played. We both played the piano, and it was thrilling.

RH: How much do you use events in your own life to understand characters you're playing?

SEM: A lot. I can't think of anything in regard to Berniece other than the fact that we both like to keep things; she wasn't going to let go of that piano. We're not pack rats but we're very sentimental; that we definitely had in common. And the story behind the piano was important because I had family in the south who had things taken, and they were never able to recover them. The thought of family members having to struggle, and what that struggle meant, was very useful to me.

RH: How much are you affected by externals, like the costume you may wear? Do you ever get a mental picture of what the character should look like?

SEM: Yeah, but what I think is not always what the costumer thinks. And so, if there's any dialogue I try to express that. But to me it's not so much what you have on. As long as I'm not physically uncomfortable in something, I'll wear it.

RH: Have you ever had a costume that really worked for you?

SEM: Yeah, it was Ma Fletcher in *I'm Not Stupid.*

RH: And why did that one work?

SEM: Because it was so funky. And it was so *wrong.* And it's being wrong was perfect.

RH: I remember those pink high heels.

SEM: Well, she had to have pumps. This was an outfit that she felt was her at her sensual best, no matter how wretched it really was. That was a costume that definitely worked for me.

RH: Did you have a lot of say in choosing that?

SEM: I actually had seen her in a short skirt because it seemed cheaper to me. But the tight pants were more or less what the director and the costume designer had envisioned, and they worked very well.

RH: Now, Mrs. Fletcher is a woman who is clearly out of her mind. As you study a character like that, a person who's 'gone off,' do you do it any differently than you would, say, Berniece?

58

. . . with Peter Francis James in David Rodriguez' *I'm Not Stupid*, Young Playwrights Festival, Playwrights Horizons, 1991. Photo by Tess Steinkolk.

SEM: Not really. What I do is compare them: Berniece was anal retentive; she had a large stick up her behind. But Fletcher was absolutely out there; there was nothing holding her back. So for me the difference between Berniece and her was, first, for Berniece I had to physically be as tight and as closed as I could be; and for Fletcher I had to feel, 'The more out you go, the better off you are.' They were at completely different ends of the human spectrum. And I liked playing both of them for those reasons. There were things, for instance, that Ma Fletcher would do that Epatha would never do, but Epatha can live through that. And there were things that Berniece would do that Epatha would never do, but Epatha can experience that.

RH: When you did Billie Holiday in *Lady Day*, you had to learn many songs. When you learn music, what does that do for you?

SEM: It frightens the hell out of me. I believe that I'm an actor who can sing, and I would never put myself up to do something that is really all about the singing. I had some major anxiety attacks getting to that one. What saved me was the fact that the first song that started the show was a song Billie didn't really want to sing very much. She was so drugged out. She didn't really want to be there. So her nervousness worked in my favor. I'll always love "I Wonder Where Our Love Has Gone" for that reason. It helped me get into the whole show.

RH: Did you get to a point where the songs really helped you?

SEM: It happened more towards the end of the show, probably where I sang "God Bless the Child." There was a lot of extraneous material in the first part. So that song was a turning point for me. The song that meant the most in the whole show was "Deep Song." At the end of that song, there's no singing, just the mouthing of the words and that haunting music.

RH: You mentioned earlier that the thing that interested you in a role was the struggle of the character. What was the struggle of Lady Day here?

SEM: For her it was just to get through the night. And with that, the struggle of her whole life: her unsavory childhood; the death of her father; the death of her mother; her life with drugs; her relationships with men; being a woman in the music field, and specifically the jazz field where women were seen as whores, and then being a black woman touring with white bands in the South. She was in constant struggle. Looking at it as an actor, well, it was incredibly juicy material.

RH: In a show like that where it's really you and the piano player, was there freedom for you to change things?

SEM: Yeah, there was. If I got a new take on a song, I could certainly try it. That happened, really, more at the end of the run. It took me that long to be comfortable with the vocal end of it, and it only happened with "God Bless the Child" because that's really where the show had its most meat.

60

RH: Well, it was a fine performance. I liked it so much I saw it three times. What are you looking for from a director in rehearsal?

SEM: Trust. I think *trust* first, then guidance of some kind. Also, I want the third eye watching all the time. But really, first and foremost for me is trust. Because I believe that you hired me because you think I can do the work.

"Actors get to express things—even if it's through another person—that most of us would never even admit to. That's why it's so liberating. No matter what it is . . . those opportunities to deal with the darker side of your psyche really excite me."

RH: What was Lloyd Richards like in rehearsal?

SEM: Very quiet. Lloyd would only speak when he felt you were going in the wrong direction. And that I appreciated. Because at that point I was in a situation where I felt it was sink or swim. It was happening so fast. So, just let me see if I can walk through this. And he was very good that way. And then there were times he'd say to me, "I don't think so, Epatha."

RH: What's a situation you've been in with a director that wasn't good for you, and why?

SEM: Someone who doesn't trust me; someone who, no matter what I do he's not going to let me see it through to find out if it works. And I also don't want the director who absolutely believes everything I do. That's just as detrimental.

RH: Well, of course it would be.

SEM: That feeling of 'Oh, let's leave Epatha alone. She'll be fine.' It may seem like an offhanded compliment. But I'm also a part of this whole, and I'd like the same attention being given to other actors. And that has happened before, where a director will just think everything I do is golden. And that's bullshit!

RH: What's the best experience you've had?

SEM: There have been many. It's hard to pick out one. *Piano Lesson* was one. *I'm Not Stupid* was a very good experience.

RH: What made *I'm Not Stupid* good?

SEM: It was part of the Young Playwrights Festival. Here were these incredibly rich characters written by a seventeen-year-old kid, David Rodriguez. Ma Fletcher was so complex that the sky was the limit with what you could do with it. It was absolutely liberating to be so unconcerned about anything. And I was really sorry that we couldn't run it longer. It's the kind of role you need to do for more than thirty performances because you keep finding so many new things about her. You know, as we live our daily lives, we have to be so contained. In that part I was able to be so unconcerned that for Epatha it was a wonderful thing.

RH: Now, Seret Scott directed that. Where was she useful to you in finding Mrs. Fletcher?

SEM: Everywhere. I have to say that Seret was the one who allowed me to go full throttle. She'd say, "Oh no, don't hold that in. Let it out." And just in terms of the journey of the character, she was helpful in my finding and showing the breakdown of this woman.

RH: Charles Durning said, when I interviewed him a few weeks ago, that there was this ugly black pit inside all of us filled, as he described it, with sulfuric acid. And every once in a while you get a part where you have to pull up on that pit, and though it was hard, he implied that it was liberating. Was there something like that in your playing Mrs. Fletcher?

SEM: Absolutely. She's probably the ugliest person I've ever played—embittered, I mean, she killed her own son with a hammer—really cancerous inside.

RH: Do you think that playing a character like that is one of the reasons you want to act?

SEM: Oh, yeah. To be able to express that stuff with some kind of style, or form. Actors get to express things—even if it's through another person—that most of us would never even admit to. That's why it's so liberating. No matter what it is—if it's something as tight and closed off as Berniece or as far removed from that as Ma Fletcher—those opportunities to deal with the darker side of your psyche really excite me.

Photo by David Rodgers.

A Skin I Can Crawl Into

TERRY KINNEY

This interview was the first in the series for *Conversations in the Wings*. It took place on Wednesday, January 2, 1991, in my midtown Manhattan apartment. Terry, who is one of the founders of the Steppenwolf Theatre Company of Chicago, was very eager to discuss the way he works as an actor. And his way of talking about acting is completely in keeping with what you see on stage: It is impassioned, yet precise; it is emotional and yet has a thoughtful, steady control. I find Terry's way of talking about acting irresistible, first because it is so thorough and carefully thought out, but mostly because it is fueled by a great passion for and love of the theatre itself.

Roy Harris: When you read a script, what is it that makes you feel, 'I've got to do this?'

Terry Kinney: I think it changes from role to role. But I have this theory that actors have one essential statement that they tend to make all the time, not that they play the same character over and over. It's a statement about themselves while it's also a statement about a character. So usually I try to pick roles that say something I believe in, I'm eager about, and also sort of frightened of.

RH: What is your statement?

TK: Oh gosh, I don't know. When I direct, I tend to know the kind of statements to make, and the plays tend to reflect my views, but when I choose acting roles, well . . .

RH: Is it really a kind of gut response?

TK: Yeah. But, you know, heh, it's good writing that usually attracts me. For instance, when I played the lapsed preacher, Jim Casy, in *Grapes of Wrath*, I was in the middle of a kind of career crisis; I wasn't feeling a spiritual attachment to anybody. What better way to deal with that than to play someone who's gone off into the desert wanting to find it? So Casy's struggle reflected something that I felt at the time.

RH: Have you ever played a character that you really didn't like, but you liked the play as a whole so much?

TK: Uh huh.

RH: Can you give an example?

TK: Yeah, I think that's been true a lot at Steppenwolf. I took the role of the older brother in *Orphans* because Gary (Sinise) believed that he could get something out of me emotionally that I had never done before. But I remember being much more attracted to the younger brother, and it was because he was on the side of right. I think I didn't want to admit this darkness in me.

RH: It's interesting that you mention the darkness. I was going to bring up something related to it later. You did something with a kind of darkness with the minister in that TV miniseries *Murder Ordained*. You took a character that an audience can't feel much for and you made us sympathize. Does that darkness intrigue you about a character?

TK: Well, really, I played that character because I knew I could come at it from an opposite viewpoint. Try to make the guy have all good intentions with that tragic flaw of no moral code and no common sense.

RH: Okay, let's go back a little. Once you know you're going to do the role, what sort of work do you do before the first rehearsal?

TK: Well, it depends on the role, but yeah, I do a lot of homework. If I'm playing a cop, I try to hang around cops because there's a code of behavior for certain professions. You let go of this when you start rehearsing, but you want to pick up some of that energy beforehand. The other thing is, the practical research that everybody does: if I'm

66

supposed to have a southern accent, I try to really have a hold on it before I do the first reading because I don't like to waste time in rehearsal, mine or anyone else's.

RH: Well, I remember when we did *Sweet Bird of Youth*, you had a southern accent the first day of rehearsal. It changed along the way . . .

TK: Oh, yeah, sure.

RH: And when we did *Tuesday's Child*, you came in with the Irish accent and all the lines were learned. Do you often do that: learn the lines before?

TK: Yeah, I do. When I direct, I like it so much when the actors come in very familiar or off the book, because I like to get things on their feet soon. Sitting around the table is very important in terms of looking at the page, seeing the intended punctuation, etc. Ultimately, though, I like to be very familiar before I speak the character.

"I guess my constant expectation of other actors is that we will form characters and our relationships (and thus the shape of the play) in the space between us, not just in our own spaces."

RH: Okay, so we've now had the first day of rehearsal, we've read through the script, Equity's come and gone, and tomorrow you're going to work on Act I, scene 1. What would you do to prepare for that?

TK: Well, I read the scene in order to get some idea of the shape of it. You never know where the director's going to take it, so you don't want to conceptualize the character to the nth degree, but I try to get very familiar with the dialogue and other practical issues. If there's dialect, for instance, I write an entire script phonetically, usually. Also, it just helps me learn the lines.

RH: What are you looking for from other actors in rehearsals?

TK: Good question. Well, I don't come in with many conscious expectations of other people. I'm not secure enough. I know the few times I've gotten disappointed early in rehearsal is when an actor seems to be playing off of himself, or forming a character without the need for me in the scene. I guess my constant expectation of other actors is that we will form characters and our relationships (and thus the shape of the play) in the space between us, not just in our own spaces.

RH: Have you ever been in a situation where you were getting so little from another actor that you had to talk about it? Have you ever said to another actor, "Something's just not happening here?"

TK: I always feel there's a problem with me when another person is not giving. So I usually ask, "What can I do?" and I bring it up in a collaborative way. I try not to be too divisive or stand up on a soapbox about my rights.

RH: What's the best relationship in rehearsal you've ever had with actors, a situation where you got what you wanted?

TK: Well, sometimes I've surprised myself and everybody else in the room by butting heads with people and then forming a great relationship out of that. Well, Kevin Anderson and I, ever since we worked together for the first time, knew that we worked in similar ways. We like to jump in and start flailing at each other right away, taking big risks right away. So I suppose my most satisfactory relationship has been with the people at Steppenwolf, because we have that familiarity right away.

Usually the first two weeks of rehearsal are spent getting to know each other and the various work processes. Most often in theatre acting you have the time to shed ego and really start to relate to each other. In film, you come in with a lot of baggage, and most of it doesn't have time to go away. I think in film that's why some people form off-camera relationships right away.

RH: I guess it can help.

TK: Well, it supposedly helps. I'm not convinced that it does. I keep my work with actors very much in the room.

RH: Have you ever had a situation where you were working with an actor or an actress that you never felt was solved?

Terry Kinney with Paul Guilfoyle in the Second Stage revival of Michael Weller's *Loose Ends*, 1988. Photo by Susan Cook.

TK: Yeah, there are plenty of occasions. I can't think of one right now.

RH: I'll mention something I observed, and the point of this is not to talk badly about someone. When I saw *Loose Ends*, I felt there was a coldness, or what seemed that, in the actress that you were working with. Did you feel a difficulty there?

TK: Not with the actress per se. One of the issues we had in the rehearsal period—and I think this is why you saw what you saw, and it's true what you're saying—she didn't feel akin to the way the character related in that aggressive, sexual fashion, and she did not believe in the choices the character made. She argued against the woman's choices.

RH: You bring up something that fascinates me. Let's say you're playing a character and his choices are really steep, and you feel that you would never do that. In order to make it work, do you have to find a way to believe in it yourself, even if it's execrable?

TK: So often you hear actors saying that you have to love yourself in character state. I don't necessarily believe that's true. Not everybody likes themselves in life. In a case like the minister in *Murder Ordained* that you mentioned earlier, where choices are very steep and morally questionable, I think you have to make yourself believe that that's your only option. It's a desperation level, and it's starting with an emotional state that most of us don't get to experience much. You just keep raising the stakes. And I think that's how I did it with him.

RH: A question that comes up with that fellow is, why didn't he just divorce her?

TK: Oh no. I would lose my ministership, and that was unconscionable. I made his stakes so that there was no other option but to kill his wife, and that it pained him grievously to do it. So, in a way, he wasn't without conscience. In his mind, the greater good was being served by murdering his wife. He had a very direct, one-on-one relationship with God. To make that believable, you really can't judge it while you're doing it.

RH: When you are working on a role early on in rehearsal, do you ever get an idea of how this person should look? how he should dress, the weight of shoes, you know?

TK: Yeah, sure.

RH: Could you give an instance?

TK: There are many actors who start from the inside and work their way out. The way they dress, the way they walk, the way they talk; all that will come after the soul has been established. Then there are actors like Laurence Olivier who supposedly start with a cane, or a nose, or a hairpiece.

I think I have a very bastardized version of both. I'm not a technician in the Olivier respect. I may have the lines and the accent down at first rehearsal, but I'll be just as empty as one can possibly be until I find some sort of soul. But at the same time, I usually can picture the person. I like to create a skin I can crawl into. That's what makes the people I play different from me. I think about all that stuff, you know: the way a person's voice is pitched. And, of course, the way they dress, and I try to dress that way in rehearsal.

70

. . . with Joanne Woodward in Williams' *Sweet Bird of Youth*, Royal Alexandra Theatre, Toronto, 1988. Photo by Garth Scheurer.

RH: I remember the jacket you brought to rehearsals for *Sweet Bird of Youth*. It was sort of shabby.

TK: I guess I chose it because it helped me feel his shabbiness. He'd been around.

RH: In another direction for a while: what are you looking for from a director? This is a vitally important thing.

TK: I remember somebody asking William Hurt that question once. He said something, and it resounded for me. It's just so dead-on to what I feel about directors. And the word he used was *sanction*. You want to believe that you're the only choice, that they want you to explore and that they *sanction* you to take every risk you can take, and they want to push you further than you've ever been pushed before. They're not afraid of you, and you have no reason to be afraid of them. There are a lot of issues there—*trust* is a very serious one.

71

RH: What makes you trust a director?

TK: Vision. Even if it's not the one I have in my own mind. If he or she has a strong vision of the play, and there's a lot of room for me to do my work within that vision, I will give myself completely over to it. If the director has not formed any opinon of the piece whatsoever, then I start losing trust, and I think I go off on my way too much.

The best director I've ever had, and I've worked with him several times, is Gary Sinise. One reason is because he knows where I've been, where I've traveled. He knows everything I've done and how to push me further than that. He challenges me in the same way a good parent will sanction their child and hopefully create an atmosphere in which they can grow up to be their own person, independent of the parent. At the same time, the parents share their values, the things they struggled through in life and got to. They share those enough to let the child feel safe. So, *safety* is another thing.

RH: Have you ever had a relationship with a director where you felt you were on your own?

TK: Oh yeah.

RH: How did you deal with that?

TK: It happens more in television and film. I've been in situations where the directors know their camera work and know how to light a scene, but have no idea of the shape of it or how to relate to actors. So I've had to go off on my own. I tend to collaborate with the actors I'm playing with in order to shape the scene. But I'd be hard pressed to find a case where that's really worked.

RH: How particular do you like a director to be with you, moment by moment?

TK: Well, if I'm working on something I would hope that somebody would notice. You know?

RH: Of course.

TK: There have been moments when a director pushed me way before I was ready. Nikos Psacharopoulos is an example of that. I admired him. We butted heads in a good way, all in all; but, sometimes he would push

72

me towards a result when I didn't know yet how to get there. And I could do it because I think I'm a good enough actor that I can deliver on the spot.

The problem is there's usually major, specific aspects of the character and soul life missing. You know, when you see a situation like that, it's acting bravado, but in time you wonder why it doesn't move you. And it's because the big questions have not been answered.

RH: Did you enjoy working on *Sweet Bird*?

TK: Oh, I loved it. First of all, working with Joanne, and then getting to explore Williams. The language. And you know, for me a large part of the process is when you put it up in front of people, and you see what you've got. A situation like *Sweet Bird of Youth*, in which we were fortunate enough to be able to work on it while we were running. When Paul (Newman) came in and talked to me, with that vast knowledge, of all he'd been through with the piece twenty-five years before, it was incredible. He gave me knowledge of the issues he had already dealt with. He wasn't inflicting any of his Chance Wayne on me.

RH: Oh, no. I saw what was happening. It was fine. One actor educating another.

TK: He was trying to push me further in terms of exploring the litera-ture. *Grapes of Wrath* was another situation like that. We never stopped rehearsing that piece until we closed it.

RH: *Grapes of Wrath* was an incredible experience. I saw it right before it opened, and then went back several months later. And it had grown. It hadn't just become a run, after the Tony Award and all the praise. It was richer emotionally.

TK: Well, I think one of the things that happened was that we knew going in that we had a very short time. We had a final draft but the read-through lasted four-and-a-half hours. We knew there would be some *gentle cutting*. By the time we previewed in Chicago, we didn't know which way the truck turned, or anything like that. And we certainly hadn't established our characters. Actually, when it opened in Chicago we took some pretty severe criticism for the work done on it. We listened to the critics and their reservations, but we had our own before we opened the thing. What we had to do was put our egos on the back burner and go back to the drawing board. We wanted to make this work, to have more life after this run.

What we did was go back into rehearsal to the full extent. In fact, we would have rehearsed more if Equity had let us. We rehearsed every day. We kept cutting and adding and asking ourselves: what is it that moved us so much when we read that book for the first time? Why did it seem to be about us? Why was the Joad family's journey our journey? And why isn't it here yet?

Basically, we knew where the culprits were: we had far too much music and too many other alienating factors. We just had to pare it down to what the essence was. In the same way that Peter Brook starts with a raw space and puts things in as he needs them, we kept paring away. And the simpler it got, the more complex it felt. The story itself has so much emotional reverberation that, of course, you could keep on working on it.

RH: It was certainly an emotional high point for me. Let me ask you this—I almost hesitate because there's so much fakery on this subject— but, do you think there's a true place for critics in the theatre?

TK: Yeah. Like you, I've had a lot of backstage and back-of-bar conversations, too.

RH: Yeah, and some of them not very pleasant, or honest.

TK: Well, there are those critics who are unconscionable in terms of how mean they can be. They can really stop the process by attacking people's soft spots and their basic talent. To listen too much to criticism is a mistake, but with none at all, you're working in a vacuum. There's a need for audience and there's a need for critics, and there's a need for people who analyze theatre on every level. I happen to think that Frank Rich, for instance—who is the most powerful critic in the country— writes remarkably beautiful prose.

RH: I agree.

TK: He's moved me with his writing. I admire his mind. And in that regard, I think there's a need for him, and I'd be sad if he weren't writing for the theatre. There have been several occasions, however, where a

. . . with Gary Sinise in the Steppenwolf Theatre Company production of *The Grapes of Wrath*, Cort Theatre, 1990. Photo by Peter Cunningham, courtesy of Shubert Archive.

review of his has made me very eager to see a production, and the payoff wasn't nearly as good as his writing.

You know, everybody has their own opinions. It's a very subjective business. And I think that having differing opinions about things makes it clear that we do need critics. If two people disagree completely, for me it doesn't say that criticism is bogus and unnecessary. It means that all of us should go see for ourselves.

RH: How much do you listen to what critics say about your work? Let's say you read the reviews of something you've done . . .

75

TK: Well, that would be hypothetical because I don't.

RH: Oh yeah, I remember now that you don't. Well, I'll put it this way. Often, you get into previews and you're working on it during the day and playing at night. How much are you affected by what your friends say?

TK: Well, I have an ego like anyone else. When I find people unmoved or more interested in dinner than the play, or just not interested in the evening that they've seen, I get panicky like anyone else. I want to shake up people's perspectives. Maybe that's all we can ever aspire towards. And if we're not doing that, it's good that people come to previews; it makes you go back in the next day a little less self-satisfied.

The danger for me comes when people treat the work as if it's a complete thing: "It's the most moving thing I've ever seen in my entire life," and you're not done working on it. And all of a sudden you relax a little too much. It's a danger.

RH: This leads me to another question: Have you ever been praised by friends, or critics, for a performance that you felt you really weren't very good in, or weren't anywhere near what you wanted?

TK: Oh yeah.

RH: What do you do about that?

TK: It's the same as when I get criticized for something that I'm good at. I just directed a production of Craig Lucas' *Reckless* at Steppenwolf. I felt it was a statement that I believed in, and I was very satisfied with it. I loved watching it. At the opening night performance, with several major critics around, I laughed very comfortably at my own work and cried and experienced it as an audience member. But when the critics responded so negatively, it rubbed me in a very bad way. I felt they had really missed something. If you're going to believe that's possible, then you're going to have to believe also that sometimes they're going to praise you for something that you're not very pleased with.

RH: Well, let's switch tracks for a bit. What do you think is the chief difference between acting on stage and acting for the camera?

TK: A lot of people draw a very bold line between the two. I don't. I believe in verisimilitude in every form, intimacy in every form. But I

76

think a major difference is that there's no sustained work in a film, and you have to sustain your character and the emotional life of the character sitting around a set with a lot of doughnuts and crew members.

RH: In film, how do you deal with shooting out of context? What do you do in your mind to make it work for you?

"A camera does one thing that doesn't happen in the theatre, and that is it can read your mind. You can think something, and it will record that. That's a big difference, and it's a big opportunity."

TK: Well, ultimately you have to come in prepared to do the entire thing. You're shooting in the dark a bit, but what you're calling up is your own ability to summon your angels and demons at the drop of a hat. A camera does one thing that doesn't happen in the theatre, and that is it can read your mind. You can think something, and it will record that. That's a big difference, and it's a big opportunity. You blink your eyes in a close-up and it says worlds. If you blink an eye on stage, chances are it may not even be seen.

You know, it's a fallacy to think that you have to size things down for film. If you do nothing, the camera sees nothing. But the truth is more soul truth, and you really have to be naked in front of a camera. Verisimilitude is not something you can create from the outside in. You have to think it, believe it, and emote it.

RH: What is the best film experience that you've had?

TK: You know, it's really interesting. Obviously, I got a chance to develop a character doing *Thirty Something*. I always refer to that character as a sort of male bimbo. They were somewhat reticent to give me character development because they knew I wasn't going to be there for too long. It's like a bad relationship: you know you're not going to be in it in a few years. Nothing comes from it, but you still put something into it.

You know, to play the same person seven times over a several month period, I reached a comfort level in front of the camera that was invaluable to me in terms of experience. It was really a very important thing. So that was a good experience for me. Besides, it was pretty good soap opera writing.

RH: What is the most satisfying performance you've ever given?

TK: I suppose it's Jim Casy in *Grapes of Wrath*.

RH: Is that because, related to what you said earlier, it was a role that came to you at a time when you yourself needed that?

TK: Yeah. The older I get the more I have a need for a spiritual bond between myself and the play. I think it's very important for characters, well, for this country itself, to deal with spirituality. In *Grapes of Wrath*, I got a chance every night to talk about the things that we all struggle with every day, and I never felt less than one hundred percent committed and emotional. I think I've had a few very satisfying experiences, though. There was *Orphans*, which was a sort of purging experience.

RH: It was terribly purging for everyone. I was surprised how strongly I related to it.

TK: Well, which of us has not felt abandoned? *Orphans* gave me a chance, to, quite literally, scream my pain about loneliness. It was also very satisfying holding it in for an entire performance, because I always had that payoff. There were times when I was in the eighth performance of the week at the end of the fifth month, and I felt, 'I cannot do it. I can't. I can't. I can't.'

RH: So how did you make it happen?

TK: Well, you know it's the first time that these particular people have seen it, and Kevin Anderson, John Mahoney, and I made a pact with each other: if anyone was letting down, someone else would shake him up. We were very good about helping each other out in that regard. Also, Gary had made it very clear to us, never, never do less than that. And his words were with us all the time.

RH: Well, we're sort of talking all around a topic, and you've implied an answer to it, but how much do you consciously use happenings in your own life as you work on a role?

78

. . . with Kevin Anderson in the Steppenwolf Theatre Company's production of Lyle Kessler's *Orphans*, Westside Arts Theatre, 1986. Photo by Susan Cook/Martha Swope Associates.

TK: Oh, I always do. And when there's very little to draw on in the script, I create bonds between the material and my own life because that's all we have to use. Again, we're going back to all of us having one essential statement to make. I draw very, very consciously on events and feelings from my own life. Maybe I can even resolve some things in my life through the play a bit.

RH: Have you ever felt that playing a character helped you to understand your own life in some important way?

TK: Yes, I think so. It goes back to *Orphans.* For years at Steppenwolf, I was the *angry young man*, you know. Well, at the time I did *Orphans*, one reason I didn't want to play that role was I thought I had gotten rid of all that anger. But doing that character and getting in touch with my anger again, I found that it wasn't as big an issue in my life. I didn't need to act out on it in so many ways. I didn't have to get as upset with the phone company or with things going on in my marriage, because every night, I had a vehicle in which to vent my spleen. I don't think it's an ideal situation, and I don't think it works one hundred percent. You have to stay very much in tune with the story that you're telling.

RH: With you, though, this is a conscious thing.

TK: Well, no, acting, while it's happening, is very unconscious. I don't make choices while I'm acting. The conscious thing happens before.

RH: You know, an image I have of you that's very vivid is Fick slumped over that bar in *Balm in Gilead.* It's an image that remains.

TK: Well, one thread that runs through Steppenwolf Theatre Company is an attraction to people from the underbelly of life. Laurie Metcalf and I used to joke that we all had affinities towards side shows, freak shows. I feel very close to and sympathetic with people that most people would push away. I try to give them a secret, something noble about them. You know when I walk in my neighborhood on Second Avenue and see someone screaming obscenities, you have to wonder, 'Who is he? Has he driven himself insane because he couldn't deal with the world around him?' In *Balm in Gilead*, I felt an affinity for Fick because he was funny and helpless and miserable, but I also felt that at one time he had been a very vital person. That's why he needed somebody to listen to him. He was probably once a very sociable, very likable person. For whatever reasons, he had driven himself to the bottom, and he was, well, not content but resigned to it.

RH: Would you rather act or direct? I know you do both very well.

TK: Oh, act, hands down! I prefer acting a thousandfold. To tell you the truth, I hate to direct. There are only a few plays I feel the need to tackle from that point of view, and they're few and far between. I don't like making other people's decisions, don't like being a psychoanalyst. I prefer being in the chair. And I don't like the weight of the evening on my shoulders. I like to create characters, so I prefer acting.

RH: Well, you know how much I admired your production of . . . *And a Nightingale Sang.*

TK: Well, one of the reasons I wanted to direct *Nightingale* was that it was a real challenge just to figure it out. It was all dialogue, and all of a sudden she was standing on the steps of the hospital. She was in her house, and she says, "When we got to the hospital . . ." I would never direct O'Neill. There are those long, long passages of stage directions, how the next scene should be played, and I can't bear that kind of work being done for me. With *Nightingale*, I would read and say, "How the hell did she get to the hospital?" That was exciting, so it was just as creative as acting.

RH: Well, I'm dying to ask you about a moment in *Nightingale*. I asked Joan Allen once, and she couldn't remember. It's near the end of the play. Norman has just told her that he's married and has a child and must go. They're on the bench, and she crumbles the cookie.

TK: She couldn't remember that?

RH: Well, I said to her, "Did you do that, or did Terry ask you to do it?" and she said she didn't remember.

TK: Well, that's how great an actress Joan is. The answer is: both. She held this cookie every night, and we were talking about the end of the relationship and what it might do to Helen's subconscious. I remember telling her to just squeeze the cookie. And whatever happened, happened. But she kept it as an unconscious gesture, and we never discussed it after that. It was a direction, but it was an actor's genius that made it work.

RH: I never forgot it. Since you're both an actor and a director, I'll ask you: why do you think the actor/director relationship is so important?

TK: Well, as a director, what you want to be able to do is free people's impulses, give them the license to fix their own problems, courage to move out of one area into another.

RH: Let's say you're directing something; it's in previews and in basically good shape, and an actor comes to you and says, "I don't know what I'm doing." What would be your first response?

TK: I usually end up asking them questions at that point. Questions that would challenge the plateau that they're on, encourage them to think that there are choices outside of the one they're now making. If they're stuck, I'd ask questions to show that the reason they're not solving the problem is they're only thinking one way about it. I'll try to find the source of it through questions. It's really important for an actor to feel that he's come up with the source of the problem and, quite frankly, with the right questions, they have.

RH: As an actor, have you ever had to do something on stage that you didn't want to do? Something that was hard for you?

TK: A lot of times, sure.

RH: I don't even know what I've got in mind. It just popped into my head.

TK: Well, I had to be nude in *Loose Ends*, and I'd never done that. In order to do it, I had to do it in rehearsal, and let the giggles happen and let everybody see my penis. I had to get over that in front of people.

RH: Was it different being out on the stage with the lighting?

TK: I didn't have a problem with it then. It was much more difficult the first time I took my underpants off in the rehearsal room. It was humiliating. It had nothing to do with the scene. And here was this kind director saying, you don't have to do it until we're in front of an audience. But I knew that wasn't going to solve it for me.

RH: Did you get to a point where it was okay?

TK: By the time we got to performances I was basically all right. Of course, there are those things that go through your mind. You want to be accepted and you think people are really just looking at one thing. Unless the life of the scene is more powerful, then your thoughts will go that way.

82

RH: I mostly hate nudity on stage and in films. It's really a making up for the lack of something else. But it must have been okay there because I don't even remember it.

TK: Very often it hasn't got anything to do with telling the story. It's added on as atmosphere. It's often superfluous titillation.

RH: Can you think of anything we've left out?

TK: Not that I'm aware of. It's good that you're doing a book of this kind because theatre is such a dying form now. It's ironic that when you called and asked me to do this interview, I was considering getting out of the business. I'm upset about the state of the theatre. You know, I was in Paris and saw the best thing I've ever seen on a stage. It was Peter Brook's *Tempest*, and it was great because it was absolute, total theatre. I didn't understand a word of it because it was in French, but I sat there and cried the entire evening because I knew that theatre was alive somewhere in the world. We don't have a system here anymore that really supports theatre because of our economic structure. It's so sad.

Photo by Bob Newey NYC.

All These Images

MARCIA JEAN KURTZ

Marcia Jean Kurtz is probably the least recognizable name in this book. She is, however, one of several hundred actors who live and work mostly in New York, and who continually give superb, sometimes unsung performances on- and off-Broadway. Marcia Jean has always brought a luminous humanity and an offbeat edge to every character I've seen her play—from the drugged-out streetwalker in the 1971 film *The Panic in Needle Park* to her remarkable performance as a battered wife on an episode of the television series *Law and Order* a few seasons back. This interview took place in the stage manager's office of the Vivian Beaumont Theater at Lincoln Center on Friday, May 7, 1993. She was directing a one-man piece by the actor Evan Handler called *Time on Fire*, which was about his battle with leukemia. It was in previews at the Second Stage Theatre and opened a few days after the interview.

Roy Harris: When you read a play and say, "I have to do this role," what makes you feel that?

Marcia Jean Kurtz: Well, the theatrical energy is so strong, it just jumps off the page at you. You know you can dive right into the text; it's playable, and it's going to feed you and it's going to make you active. So there are no *if*'s, *and*'s, or *but*'s about it: this is the part for you.

RH: When you first read for Miss Belzer in *When She Danced*, did you know you wanted to play it?

MJK: Oh, I said, "I have to play this."

RH: What made you want to play her?

MJK: Well, it does vary from role to role, I think. But I felt I understood this woman's heart immediately. It's something that's hard to articulate, but it goes to some emotional center in yourself. You know, I knew I understood her deeply, immediately. And I knew, too, that my particular sensibility fit this character.

RH: Well, that was clear very early in rehearsal. Now, you played Belzer early in 1990 and about six or seven months before you played the mother Doris in *The Loman Family Picnic*. Did you know you wanted to play her when you first read it?

MJK: Absolutely. They are diametrically opposed characters. Completely different: a mother in the Bronx in 1965 whose son is about to have his bar mitzvah and this mysterious woman from somewhere in Russia who wanders into Isadora Duncan's home in 1924 Paris. Yet they are so completely realized by the writers Donald Margulies and Martin Sherman. Doris was so fully felt that she was a character I knew I could bring forth.

RH: Do you think you respond more to the character itself or to what the play is about as a whole?

MJK: Oh, it's a combination, definitely.

RH: One of the things I found interesting about Belzer was that you have to speak Russian and English, but English with a Russian accent. Did that intrigue you?

MJK: Very much. I think it's easier to play characters who have a defined way of speaking.

RH: Why?

MJK: I've found from teaching that, when my students do not go to the language and the rhythm of the speech, they don't know what to do with it. A person has to come from somewhere, and how he speaks is really about where he's come from. If the writer is very good, he's picked up something about the speech pattern of an area, and that pattern will help fulfill the character.

RH: Did learning Russian, and then having to speak it in the play, do something to you that doesn't happen when you speak English?

86

Marcia Jean Kurtz with Michael Miceli in the Manhattan Theatre Club's production of *The Loman Family Picnic*, 1989. Photo by Gerry Goodstein.

MJK: Yes, it made me freer.

RH: In what way?

MJK: I don't know what it is but when I am playing something that is far away and that challenges me, I feel liberated to go in more poetic directions than I might otherwise. The more definition there is, the more creative you can be.

RH: We're in the midst of a question I was going to ask anyway. Once you get a role, do you do any research?

MJK: When I got Belzer, I went to the library and found all the books on Isadora Duncan. I found an autobiography of a woman who was actually Duncan's translator (supposedly this person, though Martin created her really). And, I read about her growing up in a town in Russia and I had all these images in my head. I had these images of hunger in the town, I had images of being a refugee, of the bus she took to work every day, where she lived. But it was different with the mother in *Loman Family Picnic*. I think I knew her in my bones because of seeing women like her as I was growing up. It wasn't my family at all, but I had experienced that milieu vicariously through living in New York and growing up in the same era. So I hardly had to do any research. It just came.

RH: How much of your character's history do you come to before you get to rehearsal?

MJK: It depends on the character. But I do try to work out the history pretty fully before rehearsal starts.

RH: So you came to the first day of rehearsal of *When She Danced* with a whole history in your mind?

MJK: Yes. And the history changes, of course.

RH: Did Belzer's history change in any significant way in rehearsal? I know I'm asking about something that occurred three years ago.

MJK: I think that what happens is the parts that are weak for you in terms of images, internal images I mean, simply get stronger as you go along in rehearsal. You say, 'Okay, this isn't feeding me enough. I'm not reaching what I need to reach with this particular line or this particular passage, so let me search for the particular image that will strengthen it for me.'

RH: Now you've mentioned the word *image* a number of times. When does your image start?

MJK: As soon as I read it.

RH: And how important are the images to you?

MJK: Are you talking about the image you have of the character?

RH: Partly. For instance, do you start getting an image of what she looks like as soon as you read it?

MJK: Yeah, I do.

88

. . . with Elizabeth Ashley in Martin Sherman's *When She Danced*, Playwrights Horizons, 1990. Photo by Martha Swope.

RH: How important is that in the whole rehearsal process?

MJK: I think it's amazingly important. You know it's not just an image that you can paint. The images are like musical texture in your head. It sounds abstract but it has an effect.

RH: With Belzer did you have a clear idea of what she should look like, how she should dress?

MJK: Yes.

RH: I seem to remember something about the costume.

MJK: Oh, that costume. I thought it was ugly because it made me look so dumpy. I think Jess changed it; he changed the boots or something, or maybe he took it in to make it more defined. I remember I fought it because I had lost a lot of weight at that point, and he put me in that sack, and I said, "Jess Goldstein, what are you doing to me?" But he was right.

RH: Do you like to have input with the costume designer?

MJK: I definitely see it as a collaborative effort. Sometimes you just know if it's not working, if it doesn't move right. However, if you can physically convey what you're feeling through this costume, then it works.

RH: Did you feel that costume worked for you?

MJK: Yes. Something about the shape of it was very unclear. You didn't know exactly what was underneath it. That's what Jess was so brilliant at; she was such a mystery. And the costume was a mystery. Where did you ever see such a dress? In any store? No.

RH: And yet it seemed perfectly right for her. Let's go back a little. Before you start rehearsal, along with research, what sort of work do you do on the text itself?

MJK: Well, depending on the role of course, sometimes I'll work with my coach, Harold Guskin, because there's not that much time in rehearsal to deeply develop. I don't go to him with every role, but when I think it's something important and it needs another eye to help, I will.

RH: How do you work on it?

MJK: We just go through the text. You know, it's a funny thing now. I've studied for so many years that some things are second nature to me now. The things that once you plodded through line-by-line—all those technical acting terms (substitution, etc.)—have become automatic. So, more and more for me, it's trying to hook into what the writer wants. Not going back to what you want, but what the writer wants. Am I really, really conveying what this man or woman wants to communicate?

RH: When you work on the text, do you look mostly at your own role?

90

. . . the "clenched fist" in *When She Danced*, Al Hirschfeld drawing courtesy Margo Feiden Galleries.

MJK: Well, no. Very much at the other roles. In fact, I've always found it strange that people underline their own words. I underline the other parts. I think it was Uta who said once—I studied with Uta Hagen for years, she was one of my basic teachers—"The trick is to know what everybody else is doing, and that's how you discover what you're doing."

RH: Is there any role you've done that required more research than another?

MJK: I think when I was doing Joe Chaikin's production of *The Dybbuk*, I spent time out in the Hasidic community in Brooklyn. I slept over, I ate with them, I went to the synagogue with them. I read the *Kabala*, I read Jewish mystical texts, I studied with a rabbi at the Lincoln Square Synagogue. I perhaps even went overboard on it—that part made me a little crazy. I did, however, write a screenplay as a result of all that research.

You know, in my first Broadway show I played a Chinese girl. I spent a lot of time in Chinatown, and as a result I felt I was Chinese. I remember going to the movies and being the only Caucasian there, and thinking, 'Why is everyone looking at me? I'm Chinese.'

RH: Okay, we've had the first day of rehearsal, and tomorrow we're going to work on Belzer's first two scenes: her entrance and then the scene where she meets Alexandros. What sort of work do you do at home beforehand?

MJK: I think most of my work is done prior to the rehearsal period. But I do go home at night and go over the text. And I come in the next day, hopefully open to what the possibilities are. I guess what I do consistently is shore up my imagery, my internal imagery.

RH: There's that word again. I'm fascinated because no one else has used it like this. So what do you mean by shoring up your internal imagery?

MJK: Stanislavski said there's a movie running inside you all the time. If you are really in touch with the role, you contact events in the imagined history you've created for this character and whatever you're contacting you are living. There are moments in that person's life that are in your mind, and you have to be in constant contact with them. I think if you don't see those things, something central doesn't happen.

RH: When you're rehearsing, how much does the character change from what you worked out alone?

MJK: A lot, thank God. Really, at a certain point, you let go of all you've worked on and just do it. Ultimately what you hope is that since you've done all this work, you just become a vessel that the other people in the play relate to. You just jump right in with them.

"Really, at a certain point, you let go of all you've worked on and just do it."

RH: What are you looking for from other actors in rehearsal?

MJK: I don't think I really care any more, and I mean that in a generous way. When I was younger, I would think, "Why aren't they doing what I want them to do?" And that's a selfish way to be. At this point I'm interested in what anybody has to bring, so whatever it is I can work off of it.

RH: What is, for you, a good rehearsal situation?

MJK: A situation where people are open to the director, not shutting out ideas. I remember there was an actress I worked with once, and I thought the director was giving her the most wonderful things, and she was just closing herself off to all this good stuff. I was appalled that anyone would behave like that. It was awful.

RH: How much do you use things that have happened in your own life as you look for who the character is?

MJK: Well, Stella Adler suggested making a list: how am I like this character and how am I different from it? So you can use what you know and then look for the things that you don't know. So you use both.

RH: Have you ever come upon something in a character that you couldn't get and you thought, "What in my life is like this?"

MJK: Absolutely. That's the basis of what I was taught, and I always go back to that, particularly if I'm having trouble.

RH: Something I've always wanted to ask you about Belzer: I always felt that she had a secret of some kind that she could never share.

MJK: I don't think I had one, not really.

RH: Well, she had that wonderful monologue about seeing Isadora dance. And that always seemed infused with something special.

MJK: Well, you know, I was once a dancer, and it was very easy for me to imagine how wonderful it was to see Isadora dance, as if I had seen Martha Graham early in her career.

RH: One of the things that struck me as I prepared for this interview is that both Belzer and Doris have monologues. When you have to do a monologue to the audience, does it do anything different to the way you work on the character?

MJK: No.

RH: Who do you see yourself talking to?

MJK: The audience. Again, when I was first learning, I was taught, "Make up someone you're talking to. Talk to a specific person." But I don't need that anymore. In fact, I just did a beautiful Craig Lucas monologue at Circle Rep. Now, when I rehearsed it for Craig he used to laugh, and I enjoyed his laughter and seeing him so much that when I did it for an audience, I asked for the lights to be kept on. I just wanted that nakedness, and it worked like gangbusters. It was scary but it was wonderful because I could see if people were bored or interested. I could see the faces out there. More and more, you just let the technical devices you needed when you started drop away, because communication becomes the main thing. The more vulnerable you are, the more you get across.

RH: When you're working, how aware are you of what your body does?

MJK: Very.

RH: I thought so. I have another question about Belzer. She had a gesture with her left hand. She clenched her fist.

MJK: Yeah, I know.

RH: Was that a conscious choice?

MJK: I don't think so, no.

RH: I've always wanted to ask you about it because Hirschfeld caught that in his caricature of you. He saw something. What was it?

MJK: Who the hell knows?

RH: Perfectly good answer. Not exactly what I was looking for, but . . .

MJK: And you know, that's the best, when you don't know. It just comes and that's that.

RH: In the rehearsal process, what are you looking for from a director? What do you want?

MJK: A wonderful eye. Someone who knows the character but who doesn't have a truly *set* idea of it, and who is full of ideas. I like people who are full of ideas. I even like line readings if I'm having trouble. I look for intelligence the most, I think. Somebody who really knows his craft.

RH: What was a good situation with a director for you?

MJK: Tim Luscombe was very good. I felt like I blossomed under him. You know, I think I like English directors. I worked with Nancy Meckler at the Long Wharf. I worked, too, with Peter Brook. They know the work inside out. They're not fuzzy about what they would like to see ultimately. They know how to get it. And their language is very well defined. They don't put up with nonsense, and they have a wonderful sense of theatricality. It's not an iffy ballgame.

I like a director, too, who chooses well, who can say, "Oh, I like that." You know, you hire the right person for the role and then you edit them carefully. That's what Peter Brook did. He got everything from his actors because he knew how to edit them. He created an atmosphere where everyone wished to bring the best of themselves out. You used to see his back stiffen like a little cat when he saw something he really liked.

RH: Now you're directing Evan Handler in his one-man piece *Time on Fire*. What is the difference for you between acting and directing?

MJK: The biggest difference, really, is that when you go to the party after the show no one knows who you are. Seriously, for me it's not so separate.

RH: Would you rather act or direct? You can change your answer at any moment.

MJK: I think my first passion is acting. But I certainly love creating something as a director.

RH: What do you love about it?

MJK: Well, I taught for so long, and when you teach you are directing, in a way. You're shaping things, you're choosing things, you're helping another person to communicate something. Having been a dancer and a choreographer (and my other profession is photo editing), they're all about trying to find the right image—that word again—that communicates what the written word is trying to say.

RH: How much did you have to do with shaping Evan Handler's piece?

MJK: So much. Because Evan brought some eighty-odd pages, and it was thrilling but very unfinished. So much of it was about editing, and finding the pieces that would tell the story in the best way. It was very much a dramaturgical task. I like being able to shape something, and then being an actor helps because you know viscerally what works and what doesn't.

RH: How has working on Evan's piece affected you, the actor?

MJK: Well, one thing comes to mind: to me it's more and more important to trust the director.

RH: I've been in several situations where actors don't trust directors. Sometimes they're right. But sometimes actors don't trust a director and they are dead wrong. Okay, he may be imperfect, but he has a vision, and it works, and the show is going well. What do you think makes actors not trust a director when they should?

MJK: I'm not sure I know. But if you train very rigidly in one direction, and if the director's way of working is different and you won't budge, you've got a problem. If you're not open to someone else's way of working, well, that's against spontaneity. And it's bad for a show. When actors hang onto "This is the only way to work," that's where a lot of the trouble comes from.

96

RH: To change the subject a bit: what do you see as the chief difference between acting for the theatre and acting for the camera? I mean both film and television.

MJK: I don't see that much difference really. You know, I just saw a pilot I did; it was a scene with Peter Boyle. When I saw how they cut it up, oh, they just destroyed it.

RH: Do you feel that in TV you have less control over it?

MJK: I suppose. But this hasn't happened to me very much. I was surprised.

RH: Now I've seen you twice on *Law and Order*. One was based, I feel quite sure, on Hedda Nussbaum.

MJK: Yes, it was.

RH: Now, when you play someone who is based on a real person, how do you approach that? Is it any different from how you approach any role?

MJK: Well, I had two days so I didn't have much approach at all. I didn't have any more time than that.

RH: So what did you do?

MJK: Ran to my coach and went over the whole text carefully. Now I had watched all of the stuff about Hedda. I'd been fascinated by her, as everyone was. So my imagination was alive to the possibilities of the character. A lot of actors will tell you that psychotics and murderers are the most fun to play. So I just dove right in and had one of the best times of my life. The person who was most helpful to me on that was Joe Stern who was once a New York actor and is now associate producer of the show. And it was Joe I looked to after each take. And he'd give me the okay or he'd say, "Try Blanche DuBois here." Joe was my barometer on that one. I had such a desire to play that woman because of all it brought up: who was she? why did she do these things? It brings up the whole question of abused women and you have to tap into the masochistic side of oneself, and you just go for it.

RH: What made you want to play it?

MJK: She just fascinated me. The case fascinated me. It brings up so much about our society that is very troubling. And to see this middle-class, well-educated woman in publishing collapse into this totally fragmented person was an acting field day. You just take tiny little aspects of your own life, and you build her from those.

RH: Often when you shoot for TV or film, it's done out of context. Did you shoot that out of context?

MJK: Yes.

RH: How do you deal with that?

MJK: Well, that's just part of your arsenal of technique, ultimately. You know, sometimes you have to start rehearsal in the middle of a play. You still know the beginning. You say, okay, we'll do this scene now. Really you have to know the whole story.

But sometimes you do see something at the end and you say, 'If I'd gone through that, I could have played it better.' In *Dog Day Afternoon*, Pacino discovered something well into the shooting that changed the beginning for him. So they reshot the beginning. But I think because you know where you're headed and you know the emotional journey of the character, you can shoot out of context if you have to.

RH: Do you think a director's purpose in film is different from a director's purpose in theatre, or is it the same?

MJK: I think in television they leave you alone a lot more because they expect you're going to just have it when you walk in. In most of the TV I've done there's been very little rehearsal. And they cast you that way. They want to see the performance when they cast you and then they know you'll deliver.

RH: What is a favorite film experience?

MJK: Doing *Dog Day Afternoon* was great fun. Sidney Lumet was wonderful, so full of enthusiasm. He used to watch me kidding around in between takes, and he would later shoot what I had done. That's how my part got done, because there was nothing written for the bank tellers. I was joking around with one of the sound guys, pretending to do obscene phone calls, and Lumet saw it and put it right in the film.

. . . as the character based on Hedda Nussbaum, about to unchain the lock on her door, on the television series *Law and Order*, 1990. Photo by K.C. Bailey.

RH: If you could play any role written, what would you play?

MJK: What someone hasn't yet written. I love new plays.

RH: Me, too. It's the creation that's thrilling. Watching it from the first day and seeing how it changes.

MJK: I just think it's very important to keep working all the time. I get nervous if I haven't acted in a long time. But the directing seems to help me get through the dry spells. Being involved in theatre, keeping the teaching and the directing and the acting going . . . you know, as long as the creative impulses are being satisfied to some degree, I'm pretty satisfied.

Photo by Tess Steinkolk.

The Author's Intentions Are God

ROBERT SEAN LEONARD

This interview took place on Friday, May 24, 1991, on the Mainstage at Playwrights Horizons where Jon Robin Baitz's *The Substance of Fire* was playing. Considering that he is the youngest person who talks here about acting (he was 22 at the time of the interview), it is remarkable that Robert Sean Leonard speaks with so much ease and apparent knowledge on a subject that can be as elusive as this one. The clarity he has as he discusses how he works on a role is not unlike the focus he brings to the characters he creates on stage. At the time of this interview, Mr. Leonard had recently finished a run of *Romeo and Juliet* for the Riverside Shakespeare Company.

Roy Harris: So let's start at the beginning. If you get a script and you read it and say to yourself, "I've got to do this," what makes you feel that?

Robert Sean Leonard: Well, that's hard to say. It depends on if you're reading for a certain character—I mean, if you're not sure who you're going to play yet. I guess I read specifically for the author's intentions of the play.

RH: Do you ever take a role—maybe it's not so wonderful—to be a part of that writer's particular world?

RSL: Oh, yes. But if the play is important to you and that moving to you, then a small role becomes important because of what the author's saying. I'll be doing *Our Town* in London this fall and early winter. George is a very nice, I thought, young juvenile role to do. But then I read the play again, and I was astonished at the simplicity and importance of Wilder's message. Suddenly, George became much more important to me. I realized his place in that world, and it was big. If you look at the play, no one talks to each other. Except for the soda fountain scene. And there they talk. That's why they get married. Seeing this made playing him exciting. The way George has to deal with life and death is amazing.

RH: When you decided to do, for instance, the Greek pianist Alexandros in *When She Danced*, what made you make that decision?

RSL: Joanne Woodward told me I had to do it.

RH: That's a good reason; she's very smart.

RSL: Well, that play defined the undefinable qualities and questions about what I do as an actor. And I'd never seen that in a play before. So, I guess it was both things: the play itself and what a wonderful character.

RH: When you were working on Alexandros, what did you find the most challenging thing about it?

RSL: Oh, come on, Roy, you remember?

RH: Well, I have to ask you now as if I weren't there. I'm an impersonal interviewer now.

RSL: His incredible self-confidence. The guy walks into a room and you look at him. I've never been able to do that. I've seen other people who have that. And, it's not a quality you can *play*. It's not like an accent. It's a *within* quality. And you're in awe of it when you see it.

RH: Well, you have a quality as an actor of self-effacement. Do you think you had to get past that, go beyond it in some way?

RSL: Oh, yes, but what a time I had working on it. It was a breakthrough for me. Sitting at that piano, standing up and saying, essentially, "I am a prodigy." I would say it in the mirror at home and I couldn't do it. It

102

Robert Sean Leonard with Elizabeth Ashley in *When She Danced*, Playwrights Horizons, 1990. Photo by Martha Swope.

goes against everything you try to be as a human, as an actor. To never assume you know because then you'll stop growing. That was completely foreign to me.

RH: Did you feel you were the right choice for the role?

RSL: Oh, yes.

RH: Me, too. It has to do with the other quality we talked about: something reserved and thoughtful. If you don't have that, then the sureness of Alexandros will be obnoxious.

RSL: What was fascinating for me: to have an amazing bravura, and at the same time, as Quixote says, to have the humility to "love pure and chaste from afar." To love purely requires a lot of humility. It goes against the bravura. With Alexandros, I had the humility, but as you know, it took weeks and weeks to get the right assertiveness.

RH: It was fascinating watching it happen. All right, let's back up a minute. You got that role a couple of weeks, at least, before we started rehearsal. What sort of work did you do, if any, before the first day of rehearsal?

RSL: Well, the bravura element didn't even occur to me until I started saying the words out loud in rehearsal with the likes of Marcia Jean Kurtz, Elizabeth Ashley and Jonathan Walker all sitting there watching me. Actually, the thing I dove right into was the Greek accent. That sort of gives you a center. It's a tangible task. And you have to accomplish it in a certain amount of time. The accent gives you a guideline. You go to the dialect coach and you sit down and start. "No," he says, "the *A* is pronounced this way. It's always pronounced this way." It was so refreshing to have a guideline as your beginning point. Otherwise, where do you start?

RH: Did the actual pronunciation of particular words tell you anything about who the person was?

RSL: I would say the rhythm of it more than the pronunciation of it. The clipped musical rhythm gave me a sense of his spontaneous movement, his vital energy. There's a snappiness to Alexandros, which I really don't have as a person. Something happens to you when *you* get to have that snappy, clipped musical speech coming out of your mouth. You change inside.

RH: Let's say it's Thursday night and tomorrow you're going to work on the scene where you introduce yourself to the translator, Belzer. What sort of ordinary, basic work do you do on the scene?

RSL: You know, the first time this ever came up was when I was doing *Beachhouse* with George Grizzard. I was sixteen. I was up there one day doing it, you know, just doing it, and Melvin Bernhard the director said, "What are you doing here? What is this about?" And I had no clue. I was just asking my dad where the letter was. Well, he said, "Do you have any assumptions about it? Who's it from? Is it from your mother? If so, what would that mean to you?" When I went home that night, I

104

wanted to quit the business. I cried. And to this day, it's always an obsession of mine—not getting general and relying on some phony charm. What I want to do is get specific and ask myself the necessary questions: what is his intention here? what's he after? why? So, to answer your question, I read the scene, trying to pick out where they're starting, where they're heading, and how they got there. If something changes, where does it change? However, I usually find out more in rehearsal than at home.

RH: Sometimes, do you find after a rehearsal or a series of rehearsals on a particular scene that there's more there?

RSL: Oh, sure. The more you work, the more you find. You can be hitting your head against a wall, as I was with Alexandros, and the director can say, "It's because you're not as confident as he is." Like any trouble you have, once you define it, it's so much easier to deal with. Then you know what you're after.

RH: Do you try to look and see an intention in every *line*, or a basic intention in a scene?

RSL: I'm sure that you should, but I've found that there's a level of subconscious work that goes on. I find that it's much better for me to find out what's there *with* the person in rehearsal. It doesn't mean I don't think about it before though.

RH: Would you say—I'm asking a loaded question now—that you are more an instinctive actor or one more given to plan?

RSL: I think I'm more instinctive than planned, but both, I guess.

RH: From having watched you in two different rehearsal situations, I'd say you seem to have done a lot of work when you came in.

RSL: I would say that's basically true. But there are all sorts of ways of being prepared. For instance, take Romeo. My God, I spent hours just finding out what all those words mean. And then, with Shakespeare, it's so maddening because one thought can mean many different things. You don't have to choose one. Another form of preparation is just knowing your character so well—the background you've come to through what the

105

playwright made up—that when something comes up, you instinctively know what's wrong or right.

RH: When you're working on a role, do you ever get a picture of what the character should look like?

RSL: Yeah, and it's never me!

RH: Well, it shouldn't be you. You're playing somebody else.

RSL: But I never get that out of my head. I can think back on every role I've done and picture who should have played it instead of me— what type of person; what he looked like.

RH: Does it help you to do that?

RSL: Sometimes. Slowly the picture in your mind becomes you. I can look back now and say, yes, I'm Eugene Jerome. Yes, I'm Romeo. But it took a while for me to get there, to get me in the picture. It was always someone else.

RH: When you're working on a role, do you ever get a sense of how that character should dress?

RSL: Actually, not much. I know there are actors who do. I guess it doesn't matter so much. I just had a problem with that on *The Speed of Darkness*, however. The designer was very intent on including the actors in her plans. I drove her crazy. "I don't know. Why are you asking me? Whatever you put on me, I can justify." She didn't like that. But I guess it would depend on the role. The only battle I lost was she put a letter jacket on me, a varsity letter jacket. It was the only thing I didn't like. Any time I see a varsity jacket on stage, I think, 'Oh, here comes a *young* actor.' I want to be a person. It's too much a sign to me. But I ended up wearing it. She liked it too much.

RH: When you're in rehearsal, what are you looking for from other actors?

RSL: Well, hopefully we'll all be pretty solid in our agreement about what is going on in this play and what our part in it is. Of course, there are technical things: like you don't upstage someone when they're talking. An important thing is knowing when the scene is moving, and knowing

106

. . . with Len Cariou in Steve Tesich's *The Speed of Darkness*, Belasco Theatre, 1991. Photo by Martha Swope.

when it's time to take a moment for yourself. And that's hard. A lot of actors get up there, and understandably, the play is about them. If you're playing a milkman, the play is about a milkman. But when that becomes your only reality, you lose sight of the intentions of the play. You know, it's so obvious to me when an actor feels he is the most important thing in the play. It's so portentous. Every line means something. It's so boring. Maybe that's why I'm a little afraid of finding intentions in every line. Then it all gets too much *meaning*.

RH: Have you ever worked with an actor—you don't have to give a name—whom you had a problem with?

RSL: Sure. I worked with an actress in a film who had no clue, didn't know the first thing about acting. The camera would go to you, and she'd be off camera reading her next film. She would say her lines not looking at you. That drove me crazy. On stage, I must say I've never worked with anyone where there was a problem. I've worked with people who really snapped with me and then people who were just all right to work with.

RH: Who is an actor you've really liked working with?

RSL: Cynthia Nixon: when you work with her, she's so in tune with what's going on. When a scene is playing, it just lifts and rises. She's like a dancer. I love all her work. Something happens when that actress walks on stage. It elevates into another world.

RH: What are you looking for from the director?

RSL: An unshakable vision. You know when they have it, because you'll ask questions and immediately there's an answer that makes sense, and it makes sense in relation to everything that's happened so far.

RH: What if it's a vision you don't agree with?

RSL: That doesn't matter. I want a vision that's like a force running through everything.

RH: What happens when there's not a vision?

RSL: Well, my sister told me once, when she was in third grade, her whole class went into the city. When they came up from the subway, the teacher—for a moment—didn't know where she was. My sister saw that look, and suddenly was terrified. She lost all faith. And that's horrible when it happens with a director, and it can happen in an instant. If they have an unshakable vision, it won't happen.

RH: Have you ever had a director tell you something and you felt that you just couldn't do it?

RSL: Couldn't from myself?

RH: Yes.

RSL: Well, no, because the minute someone asks something of me, my first reaction is, "Goddammit, I can do this. I can do whatever they

108

want." You know, to me the author's intentions are God, and the director is the channel for those intentions. The very idea of not being able to do something a director asks, or being averse to it, is upsetting to me.

RH: Have you ever been in a situation where some or all of the actors didn't trust a director? How do you deal with that?

"Cynthia Nixon: when you work with her, she's so in tune with what's going on. When a scene is playing, it just lifts and rises. She's like a dancer."

RSL: Good question. Well, if a director can't give you an answer for why he wants you to do something a certain way, then you shouldn't trust him. If I initially don't trust a director, I try to find out why I don't. Maybe it's me. But if he can't give you an answer, you can't get bitter. You have to rely solely on yourself, or on yourself and who you're playing with. You do the best you can and hope for a short run.

RH: What director would you most like to work with?

RSL: Mark Lamos.

RH: Why?

RSL: In everything of his I've seen I always witness such clarity and devotion to the author's intent, even if it's complex, as in *Hamlet* or *The Master Builder*.

RH: For someone your age, you've had a chance to play some very good roles. What's been the most challenging role so far?

RSL: Romeo. I think I misunderstood him the whole time I was playing it.

RH: Oh, Bobby, everybody who plays him feels that, don't they?

RSL: Probably. When I took the role, I thought, I'm going to make him honorable, which I think he is. Most people feel he's a sap. My mistake was making him that way from the beginning.

RH: What do you mean?

RSL: A friend of mine said late in the run that that first scene is not about a man who knows love. It's about a kid who thinks he knows what love is. Then he meets Juliet. He said, you should make us puke in the aisles when you tell Benvolio what you think love is. And he's right. From the moment I walked on stage, boy, did I play passion. All through the Rosaline stuff with Benvolio, it was passion. Consequently, when I met Juliet, I just didn't have anywhere to go. It was like starting with a nine and getting to a ten.

RH: But you seemed to have a good time working on it.

RSL: Well, I learned from it. You need to see his feeling about Rosaline in order to really appreciate the great feeling he comes to have about Juliet. I didn't look at it intelligently enough. I didn't realize the simplicity of: he doesn't know what he's doing and then he does know what he's doing. It's also our job as Romeo to convince the audience that once he's in love with Juliet—and some people would scream at this—it's worth dying for. With all the mistakes I made, it was a great experience.

RH: Ten years from now you can do it again and think what that will be like.

RSL: I'll have a whole new series of questions about it. That's why acting is so phenomenal. You can't ever be good enough.

RH: Does there come a point for you in rehearsals, or probably in performance somewhere, where you think you got it?

RSL: No. There are points where I feel I've gotten something. I've never given a perfect performance. I wonder who has?

RH: Well, if they think they have . . .

RSL: I don't want to talk to them.

RH: Me either. Have you ever been praised by a friend for a performance that you thought was bad, or certainly not adequate?

RSL: Sure.

RH: How do you deal with that? How does it affect you?

110

. . . with Gerit Quealy in the Riverside Shakespeare Company's production of *Romeo and Juliet*, 1990. Photo by Carol Rosegg/Martha Swope Associates.

RSL: Well, you're praised very often for things that you don't deserve to be praised for. But you learn pretty quickly who does that and who doesn't. So I guess you learn who to listen to. How do you deal with it? I get very indignant. I go home and I say, 'Well, they're wrong.'

When I was filming *Dead Poets Society*, I noticed that Peter Weir (the director)—as soon as he'd say, "Cut"—would look to John Seal (the cinematographer) first. As soon as the play is done, I consider myself a cinematographer; I check with myself. Then I check with the director. A friend may be right in saying something I did was false, but I have to go by what the director is asking for. So, it's complicated when friends say things. Very complicated. It's very sacred between you and the director, and frankly, people need to honor that.

RH: What's the biggest difference between acting on stage and acting for the camera?

RSL: In some ways, they're very different and then in some ways they're not so different at all. It's a little like recording music and then playing it live. In one sense, you're part of the whole, but fragmentally. In film, you're offering pieces, and the director makes it whole.

RH: Do you prefer one over the other?

RSL: No. I don't know. I think I prefer theatre. Is that three answers?

RH: You can change your answer later. I'm trying to find out what your feeling is at this moment. In film, you go in on the first day of shooting and you may shoot pages 68–72. In terms of preparation, how do you shoot something that's in the middle of that character's (for want of a better word) journey? What do you do with all that comes before?

RSL: Homework becomes much more important in film, ironically, because in film, usually your work has much less to do immediately with other actors. It's much more a solitary art. Because you start with page 68, you have to know exactly where that character is and has been before page 68. Hopefully, the director will know, too. And you will discuss it together, as Peter Weir did with me through the shooting of *Dead Poets.*

RH: Where do you think the director is more important, or is he: in film or stage?

RSL: They're more important for different reasons in both areas.

RH: Have you ever been asked to do something by a film director that you didn't want to do, or thought you shouldn't do?

RSL: Yeah. Usually it has to do with poor writing. Sometimes the director will want something because of what's in the script, and you have to do it, even if you're not sure it's right.

RH: Let's say you did a role on stage for six weeks, night after night, and then you go and make a movie of it. A scene you've done many times, you're now going to do and the camera is going to be *this* close to you. Does it do anything to your way of thinking about it, to know the viewer is now so close?

RSL: The relationship with the director becomes much more intimate. It would be like having the director on stage with you at all times, saying, "How about this? how about this? or how about this?" They are creating

112

with you at the moment, and they know, and hopefully you do too, the journey of this character. It would be wonderful to do it on stage first because your homework would be done for you.

An obvious thing is that when the camera's so close you do bring it down, even though you try to keep it as truthful as you would anywhere. In film, you do a lot more with your eyes, where on stage you use your hands and body language.

RH: So far, what is your favorite film role?

RSL: Well, I'd have to say *Dead Poets Society* is for me in film what *Brighton Beach Memoirs* was for me on stage. It was kind of my baptism because I suddenly found myself on the set with a powerhouse of a director. It also has to do with the time. I was nineteen. Peter took me in as the leader of this gang. He had me read poetry. Also, I had to play Puck, and he wouldn't tell me which scene we were going to do, so I learned all of Puck. Without a doubt, it was the most glorious film experience. It was college for me. All of the guys, we lived together. We had a whole floor of a hotel, and we became this group of young men. We did everything together. We created together. Ethan Hawke and I used to practice scenes listening to Beethoven's Ninth.

RH: What is your favorite scene there?

RSL: Well, for personal reasons, the scene with Ethan on the roof where we throw the desk set off. We came up with that scene. Originally, it was a scene which ended very sadly, with Ethan saying his parents didn't love him. Peter pulled us aside and said, "Okay, we know all this. Let's just have a scene about friendship." And the three of us came up with the scene where we destroy the desk set. That was a real accomplishment for me because improvisation has always scared the hell out of me. I don't like it that much as a working technique. When the director is as strong as Peter is, then improv is wonderful.

RH: We've talked a little about this, since you and I are such fans of hers, but what was it like to play Joanne Woodward's son in *Mr. and Mrs. Bridge*?

RSL: It's funny. They're an amazing team, she and Paul. He's reserved. Though I don't know a thing about him, I like him a great deal. Joanne is—well, you know, there's a love you have for certain celebrities. I think she knew I had this huge feeling, and she takes that feeling and makes you feel comfortable. It's okay to have it. Know what I mean?

RH: Absolutely.

RSL: She embraces this feeling you have about her, and it frees you. Therefore, working with her was a dream. She's completely honest in her work.

RH: What was a favorite scene of yours in that film?

RSL: I don't know. I was so racked with his age throughout the filming—you know, when he was fifteen, when he was seventeen, when he was nineteen. But I guess it would be the boy scout scene. I was so worried that no one would buy that I was fifteen years old. I was twenty at the time, so they gave me braces to help me get a sense of youth. It helped. Really, though, it was memorable because Joanne was so wonderful in it. She did everything for us. She made us all look good. I remember during filming looking over at Paul when I don't kiss her and begin to sing. And he wasn't Paul, he was Mr. Bridge, my father, and looked at me with such hatred, and it was startlingly clear that he loved his wife more than me. For him, his son wasn't going through something; no, some guy just hurt his wife.

The most joyous scenes were coming home from the air corps through the final scene where I take her hand. For me, Douglas is the only one in that house who grows up with a true sense of other things in the world. After all, he's the one who writes the books.

RH: Well, you do feel he's the least selfish of those children.

RSL: Yes, well, I think that's evident even when he's behaving like a brat with her. I wanted people to feel: yes, he's doing it, but it's killing him to do it. I remember feeling, 'If this guy can write about these people so brilliantly and so warmly, there's got to be something there, and I'll be damned if I'm not going to get that feeling into the film.' In his air corps training, Douglas met so many different kinds of people that he was able to look at his parents objectively and with love. To me, it's the only moment in the film where anyone reaches out to Mrs. Bridge as a human being, not the mother. Actually, Paul would probably disagree

. . . with Joanne Woodward in the 1990 film *Mr. and Mrs. Bridge*. Photo by Mikki Ansin.

with this. But I guess we each see it from our own point of view in the film.

RH: One more quick thing before we close. If you could work with any actor, actress, director, and pick your own role; in other words, what's your ideal situation?

RSL: I think doing *The Seagull* with Joanne would be an amazing experience. Doing anything with Ian Holm. I've always had a dream of playing Horatio to someone else's Hamlet. Horatio to Gary Oldman's Hamlet would be very good.

Photo by Deborah Feingold.

Where Contradictions Meet

STOCKARD
CHANNING

This interview took place on Saturday, April 18, 1992, in a rehearsal room at Lincoln Center Theater. Miss Channing was between the final matinee and evening performances of John Guare's *Four Baboons Adoring the Sun* at the Vivian Beaumont. Though by her own admission she was very tired, as she began to talk any hint of that quality disappeared. Listening to her talk about how she approaches and develops a role was almost like watching her become one of the characters she has made come alive on stage: Miss Channing creates an intellectual urgency so immediate it is almost palpable. Two days after this interview, she flew to London to begin rehearsals for the West End production of Mr. Guare's *Six Degrees of Separation*.

Roy Harris: When you read a play and you say, "I want to do this role," what makes you feel that?

Stockard Channing: I'm very bad at reading plays to myself really. So I usually like to read it out loud with other people. I believe in interaction of the characters and reading it out loud gives you a sense of how it plays between the characters.

RH: When you were offered Bunny Flingus in *The House of Blue Leaves*, one of the great comic roles, what made you interested in doing her?

SC: Funny you mention that. John asked me which role I wanted to do: Bunny or Bananas. It was a toss-up. And someone said to me, "You should do Bunny because it's more lighthearted." So it was a choice between having fun or being miserable every night. So I opted for Bunny.

RH: Well, let's say you've got a month before you start rehearsal. What sort of work do you do beforehand?

SC: Other than read it?

RH: Yeah.

SC: Well, not much really. I don't think there's much point because if you make choices on your own there's a chance you'll be at odds with the production. Again, it's because of that interaction with the other actors.

RH: What is your thought process before rehearsals?

SC: Well, I'm very interested in externals, the things that I can hook onto: costume, accent, wigs, etc. And I will think about that.

RH: Do you ever get a mental picture of what the character should look like?

SC: You know, I had this photo of Kim Novak in a violet sweater that someone had given me, and that was my inspiration for Bunny Flingus. That sort of platinum hair. And Ann Roth was extremely helpful. We discussed how there are some women who are stuck in an aesthetic at the point when they felt they were most attractive. Even though the play takes place in the early sixties, Bunny, we felt, was stuck in this classic late-fifties look, sort of neo-Kim Novak. All that contributed in my mind to who Bunny was. Also, the Irish-Queens accent, of course, was very important. That was a lot of fun. It gave her a specific rhythm.

RH: When you have an accent, do you research that before you start rehearsal?

SC: Oh, yeah, of course. It's very important in defining who the character is. For instance, when I did *Woman in Mind*, the dialect coach, Tim Monich, was very helpful. She was a very specific woman from a particular London suburb—not lower class, not upper class, not cockney, but somewhere in the suburban middle. She was a minister's wife. That accent helped me define the character by telling me what limitations she had on her own existence. It was a very successful accent.

118

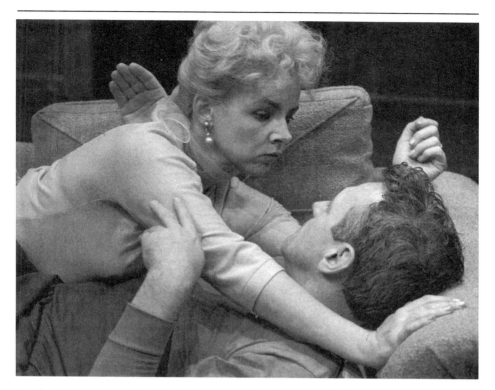

Stockard Channing with John Mahoney in the 1986 revival of John Guare's *The House of Blue Leaves*. Photo by Martha Swope.

RH: Yes. It was a different sound than you made in any other role I've seen.

SC: Yes, right. That sound was helpful in making her a specific, unique person in my mind.

RH: Do you find that when you get the costume, does that sometimes do something to you?

SC: Yes, absolutely. For instance, in *Six Degrees of Separation*, William Ivey Long did the clothes. In the initial production in the Mitzi Newhouse, we had very little time. I came into that show a week after rehearsals started. We went to Bergdorf's and we found this Armani suit and it felt right. Then we continued defining her. We decided, for instance, that she doesn't wear much jewelry. Even dressing to go out to dinner, she

119

was simple. This was a businesswoman, in that her social life was her business, not someone in an office. There was a certain European aesthetic to her. When we did the second version, when it moved upstairs to the Beaumont, that black dress was taken rather directly from John Singer Sargent's *Madame X*.

RH: You know, when I saw it, I did think, 'She looks like Sargent's *Madame X*.'

SC: That dress was a certain balance between sensuality and ladylike-ness. By that point I had found out who Ouisa was. We felt that she was taller than I was—that's why we chose the very high, Manolo Blanick heels—and she had a formal way of sitting and holding herself. And the hair (the second time when we had a good wig) was in a tight french twist, not a hair out of place. And we went after this formality as a counterpoint to her warmth. Ouisa was a very warm human being. The physicality was very important. I tried to make her as long as possible, as attenuated as possible to counteract a sort of bubbly thing she has inside. She had a certain poise about her, and she carried herself a certain way.

RH: The Sargent image is so right. There's that wonderful sense of elegance and something sure of itself.

SC: That's what we were after.

RH: And too, there's a mystery and vulnerability that that character has.

SC: Yes, she does, but it has to be offset by a certain elegance, something almost austere. This is not a practical person. Look at that creamy beige thing she wore. This is not a woman who spills her food.

RH: Well, she's not going to mop the kitchen floor.

SC: No, or do a lot of dishes.

RH: When you're in rehearsal, do you do any sort of homework each night before you come in?

SC: I don't really do a certain kind of work because I believe in that interaction among the actors. But I think about stuff a lot. I can't help

120

. . . with Courtney B. Vance and John Cunningham in the 1991 Lincoln Center Theater production of *Six Degrees of Separation*. Photo by Martha Swope.

it. I'll be walking along and something will just come to me because a character's on my mind. I don't set aside a certain amount of study time or anything like that.

RH: You've mentioned the word *interaction* several times. In the rehearsal process, what does that mean to you?

SC: What keeps people on a stage is the tension between them. I believe that the *way* people listen to each other is very important in that tension. In real life we listen, and we'll grab onto a phrase and respond to that. If you say something, I may hear one word, and I'll want to answer that. So it's the desire to speak or not to speak (which is just as strong).

So I will look to what the other person is saying, and I'll want to answer it or avoid it. Picking up cues, for example, really means hearing a word in what a person is saying and responding to that. Or not responding. And you have to pick your spots for not responding very carefully. When a person doesn't respond, or has trouble responding, or can't respond, it tells a lot about them. Being stunned and not able to talk is in itself an action.

I always look for the actions. See, that's why you can't make choices about what you're thinking at home. You've got to have the other actor there making choices with you. The two of you have to define the area together.

RH: What annoys you the most about the way another actor works? And I'm not looking to have you trash anybody.

SC: No, I know that. I would say what I don't like is when people aren't working hard enough. Because I'm looking for something I can connect with; if they're not working, then there's no connection.

RH: It's interesting you say this because four of the other people I've interviewed have all said the same thing. It was not the *way* another person worked . . .

SC: No, of course not. It's different when the person is just slow, because they're working then. Because I'm never out there alone, working by myself. I'm never *in one*. I always need the other person.

RH: What do you want from a director?

SC: Well, I basically want them to leave me alone a lot. I don't like people who intimidate me, who are bitchy, or who are out there on power trips because all that freezes me up. I like an atmosphere of play, of relaxation, discipline, too, of course—but trusting me to have my own discipline.

The director is the person who sets the tone for the whole rehearsal process. He has to deal with so many things: the designers, the producers, the crew, other actors. My responsibility is to give him or her as much as I can and to be disciplined about it. I think the director really comes most into play when he gives you a direction. For instance, he says,

. . . with Simon Jones in the 1988 Manhattan Theatre Club production of Alan Ayckbourn's *Woman in Mind*. Photo by Gerry Goodstein.

"You're in the wrong direction here. This is what I'm seeing." And you say, "Oh, but that's what I meant." "But that's not what I'm seeing. What if you went in this direction," etc. That is the kind of thing that is really helpful: showing me that I'm giving an impression that's the opposite of what I thought I was doing. We don't see ourselves when we're on a stage. The director is an outside eye. It's like seeing the dailies when you're making a film. And you say, "Oh, I see. That's the one. That's the scene that's clearest." On stage we can only do that from inside out, so we need the director to show us when it's not working.

RH: You've worked with Jerry Zaks twice, both on John Guare plays. What was he like to work with?

SC: He's absolutely meticulous. He laughs at the fact that he's so bossy. He is. He is the center, the head of the rehearsal. Because I've worked with him twice, there's an ease. I understand the discipline in which he works, and I respect it. He's very sensitive to the atmosphere in the rehearsal situation. No one goes in or out of the room unless absolutely necessary. There has to be quiet. Some directors are more easygoing. Jerry is absolutely consumed with what he calls passing the ball: telling the story of the play, not being self-indulgent.

The first time we worked together we had some moments of friction. But I never worried about that because I knew it would come. He did, too. He trusted me and I trusted him. We worked amazingly well together. Jerry's into control but it's worth it. And if he trusts you, he'll say, "Oh, I see. I get that," or "No, no, I don't get that. Try this." Tiny little things. Minute little things. An inflection or part of a word. And I like that. I like that attention to detail. I really got off on it. Particularly with *Six Degrees*, because I'd worked with him before.

RH: You mentioned earlier seeing dailies, and it brings up a question I want to ask: what do you see as the chief difference between acting on stage and acting in film?

SC: The scale of everything. How close it has to be. You know, it is a truism: for film you have to scale down the actions, at least in a realistic film. But when I'm on stage, I want it to be like seeing a film: I want to be able to transmit that intimacy and have you feel it just like you would in film, but for twelve-hundred people.

RH: When you're working in film and you have to shoot out of sequence, how do you deal with that?

SC: Well, you just do it in your head. Sort of the way you did it in rehearsal. You know, you often rehearse a play out of sequence, and yet the rehearsing makes for the continuity later. If you have the throughline in your head, and you've had a chance to sit down and read through the whole thing with the actors before filming, then it should be there for you. Shooting out of continuity is really not a problem, because I write things down. I break down a play scene by scene anyway.

RH: Do you like working in film?

SC: Oh, yeah.

RH: Do you prefer one over the other?

SC: Actually, it depends on the people, the situation, the script. You know what I mean.

"What keeps people on a stage is the tension between them. I believe that the way people listen to each other is very important in that tension. In real life we listen, and we'll grab onto a phrase and respond to that. . . . So I will look to what the other person is saying, and I'll want to answer it or avoid it."

RH: I've been watching your films in the last weeks to get a sense of the overall work, and I wanted to talk about one because I liked it so much, and frankly I didn't expect to. It's the Harvey Fierstein piece, *Tidy Endings*, one of the acts from his play *Safe Sex*.

SC: Oh, yes.

RH: I had not seen the play. When I rented it, I only knew what was written on the jacket blurb. And the film was amazingly moving to me. The subject matter, of course, but her revelation at the end, I was completely unprepared for it.

SC: Yeah, well, that's a story.

RH: You know, I'm going along watching it, thinking, 'This is a good piece of work. I like it. She's good; so is he.' And then you make this revelation, and I'm suddenly trembling.

SC: I know what you mean.

RH: I can't say how much I respect the work there. So subtle and surprising.

SC: Well, thank you. I'm very proud of the whole thing. But I've not been able to see it. Gavin Millar, the director, is one of the directors I like working with most. He's wonderful.

RH: The work was so simple.

SC: I think Harvey was very nervous at the beginning because this was a different interpretation of the material. And Gavin put Harvey at ease and got a wonderful performance out of him. What he understood so well is that in film it's all about reaction, and that's very different from the stage. Earlier in rehearsal there was a period of adjustment. By the time we got to Toronto to shoot, we were all working well together. I have a great love for that piece and for that woman. I love her strength, and showing that was all in the reactions. If you see it again, look for that.

RH: I definitely will. I know what to look for.

SC: For instance, when he describes her husband's (his lover's) death. His language is vivid. She says almost nothing. Her feeling about her ex-husband is told, I hope, in those reactions. Her response is amazingly complex, but it's in a look here, a look there. What was going on in her mind? They were lovers, they had a child. She was sitting on so much feeling.

There's a scene where she sort of blows up. And I was struck by her seeing herself as a lady. I thought, she's a lady, and she was trained not to blow up, not to release her feelings. Not that she's repressed.

RH: No, no, I know what you mean. A person with good manners?

SC: Yes, it was about manners. And so it was sort of waspy. Very different from Ouisa, because she's a woman of the everyday world. You know, someone from Rye or Westchester who had to have that kind of discipline or dignity about her. Someone sort of gracious and maybe just the slightest bit condescending. And that's where you had to start with the two of them—this well-mannered woman and her ex-husband's boyfriend. And then the fact that they bonded in that moment; it was a very delicate thing.

It's amazing to me that the whole thing takes place in that loft space. His use of the camera is excellent. It's really a conversation between two people.

RH: Well it is, and the interesting thing is that it feels quite cinematic. It's never confining in a bad sense. Other than the funeral at the beginning, the whole thing is in those two or three rooms. Now, why haven't you seen it?

SC: Well, I haven't because I had a very dear friend who died of cancer at the time. Someone I'd known since I was a child, and it reminds me so much of him that I can't seem to watch it. I know it's wonderful. It won ACE Awards, and it was popular. The irony of the whole thing was: the day that my friend died, I flew to Boston for the service and flew back. And it was the day we shot the funeral for the movie. I was so distraught and upset. But it was too much to use for the character. She was a stoic who showed little feeling, and I was absolutely a wreck. And then Harvey, who was supposed to be so distraught and show all this feeling, had just found out that they were going to film *Torch Song Trilogy*. He was in a state of euphoria, and he couldn't use that. Anyway, I'm kind of shy about watching myself. I have trouble seeing myself. It's not easy.

RH: Now, you have now done three very important John Guare women: Bunny in *The House of Blue Leaves*, Ouisa Kittredge in *Six Degrees of Separation*, and, most recently, Penny McKenzie in *Four Baboons Adoring the Sun*. Is working on a play of John's very different than, say, working on the one I saw you in while we were working at Williamstown? The Pinter?

SC: *The Homecoming*. You know, I really think the director determines the atmosphere surrounding a play. And you know, all three of those plays of John's were very different experiences: *The House of Blue Leaves* had been done before and was a proven success, *Six Degrees* was pretty much unchanged from the day I started work on it, and virtually every line of *Four Baboons* underwent some kind of change before we opened. So those things help determine the experience.

RH: Well, when you did *Six Degrees*, you did it with two different Pauls. I saw both of them. Was there any major difference in doing it with James McDaniel and then with Courtney Vance?

SC: The interesting thing about Paul and Ouisa is that we hardly ever see each other. It's a vocal thing. They were two different people, and because they were different it made the interaction different.

RH: At the end of the play, when you have that phone call with Paul, the one that begins, I think, with your saying, "You have to turn yourself in. The boy committed suicide. You stole the money."

SC: Yes?

RH: You never look at him. You're looking straight out front. He's behind and above you, being lit through the scrim. How do you approach something like that when there's no visual connection?

SC: You just do it over and over. You don't look at each other. Things sort of emerge from the repetition: thoughts, connections. You hear the questions, you answer them, and you see what happens to you. You shouldn't plan these things; you shouldn't plot them too much. Then they lose their spontaneity. It's a matter of repeating it and seeing what your imagination does with it. We just knew it had to be a very strange, circuitous sort of journey from the beginning of the phone call to the end.

RH: Another question: how much do you use things that happen in your own life over the years in preparing a role? Do you consciously say, "Oh, that's like this?"

SC: Well, sometimes, if it occurs to me. Again, I don't try to plot things too much. But sometimes I recognize people I've known or things in myself. But you know it's really a mysterious process that happens. I can't explain it.

RH: When you were working on Penny in *Four Baboons* . . .

SC: A crucial thing for me is to find where the contradictions are in the character. Where, for instance, with Penny is the contradiction? She's optimistic and is also extremely nervous. And where those two points meet is where she lives. She's strong and yet can get extremely excited and unsure. When she finds the kids in bed, her intelligence is much sharper than I thought when I first read it. She'll look at the worst possible scenario which her brain has devised in the eye. So you have someone who is strong and yet unsure. And how that works may vary from performance to performance.

RH: Where are the contradictions in Ouisa?

128

SC: There is a naivete in Ouisa which is absolutely glorious—and tremendous sincerity. Yet, she's very canny and worldly. It seems like a contradiction, but it really isn't.

RH: Oh, no.

"I don't try to plot things too much . . . it's really a mysterious process that happens. I can't explain it."

SC: It's exactly where she lives—at that point where naivete and intelligence meet. I have a favorite line of hers. It's in the scene where Paul is describing Sidney Poitier as his father, and Ouisa says: "He's married to an actress who was in one of—she's white? Am I right?" She says this without trying to be a wise-ass or anything. She has no qualms about saying that sort of thing. So she has a strange purity about her.

RH: You said a while ago that when you moved upstairs to the Beaumont that you felt you had the character. Is this what you were talking about—the contradictions of naivete and intelligence?

SC: Well, I think she was daffier downstairs. I don't know, maybe I just got more used to it. But that worldliness gave her a certain gravity. It's funny. It's a curious mix—I'm trying to think of a specific moment. When I say worldliness, for example, I mean with her kids. Because she loved them, she simply accepted the fact that her daughter couldn't stand her. She just sort of laughed at it. And that made her sort of sweet and vulnerable. There was a loneliness there that I hadn't realized was going on. And I hadn't realized it because of how giddy she was. I think she is someone who looks to have a good time without ever being vulgar. She has a great sense of sun. When she talks to the audience, she likes to laugh with them, to connect with them. But she's got a certain toughness to her as well, which Paul responds to. That's a very interesting relationship.

RH: Well, you feel there's something she sees in Paul that she's never seen in anyone else.

129

SC: Oh yeah. His intelligence. And you know, it's true—and you don't have to have a reason for it—there are those people who connect; they talk the same language. And the interesting thing: Paul and Ouisa almost never talk directly to each other. They are fascinated by each other in an almost chemical way. It's not sexual; it's not mother-son, or brother-sister. In a way it's none of these and all of them. That's why his loss is so devastating to her. Her real naiveté shows when she decides to help him and she comes up against the whole bureaucracy. Even Ouisa, in her privileged position, can do nothing about it. And it's horrifying. People are taken over by the system and some of them just disappear.

RH: Now, when you were working on Bunny Flingus, well, she's so different from Ouisa and Penny.

SC: Yes, she is.

RH: In a way, Bunny Flingus is sort of lower, or working class, Penny's in the middle, and then you've got Ouisa for whom life has been pretty easy. When you do someone like Bunny, do you think about all those kinds of things?

SC: Oh, sure. A lot of that came with the accent. That Irish-Queens is a very specific accent. I always had this thing about Bunny, and it was that sex with Artie was really not very good, and she herself was an extremely sexual being. But she was a victim of all that Irish-Catholic repression. So when she laid eyes on Billy Einhorn, it wasn't just ambition; she was just ready to come at any moment. She was just at a fever pitch inside. And the reason was that she was just so sexually frustrated. There's some dialogue in the first scene that shows this in a backwards sort of way.

RH: There is that whole thing in the first scene about how she'll have sex with him but she won't cook for him. You know, that very funny speech about "have I ever denied you?"

SC: Well, she's saying one thing, and underneath it is really something else. She says: "I took that sex test in the *Reader's Digest* two weeks ago and I scored twelve. Twelve, Artie! I ran out of that dentist office with tears gushing out of my face. But I face up to the truth about myself. So if I cooked for you now and said I won't sleep with you till we're

130

. . . with James Naughton in the Lincoln Center Theater production of John Guare's *Four Baboons Adoring the Sun*, 1992. Photo by Martha Swope.

married, you'd look forward to sleeping with me so much that by the time we did get to that motel near Hollywood, I'd be such a disappointment, you'd never forgive me. My cooking is the only thing I got to lure you on with, and hold you with."

Anyway, her uncertainty about herself came out in the screwy thing with the cooking. She was just flinging herself around that stage; she was always just touching herself, and it's because of all these repressed sexual feelings, and it all shows in her not cooking for him until after they're married. The contradiction is that because she doesn't feel she's a very sexual person and the sex hasn't been good, she's just hot to trot,

131

particularly when Billy Einhorn shows up. It's in the way she dresses, that platinum hair. She's always at an absolute fever pitch!

RH: And what a contrast to Bananas who's this ghostly vision in a soiled white nightgown.

SC: Oh, yes.

RH: Now, what was it like to work on the Ayckbourn *Woman in Mind*?

SC: It was a very difficult thing to work out emotionally. And, you know, frankly, I was well into previews before I realized really *why* she went crazy. This was a woman who all her life had blamed everyone else for what went wrong with her. And she finally realized that it may have to do with her. People used to say, why didn't she just leave him? Because she had virtually no education, no money; she was a very specific kind of English woman. She was a minister's wife; there was no money. This was no cute little English woman. I read a lot of Barbara Pym books while I was working on that to get a sense of the whole minginess of her existence.

I'd really have to have the text to show you this, but one night during a performance, I saw that for one moment she saw that it was *her*, not the people around her, and the guilt was so overwhelming that she went mad.

She was the kind of person who had no infrastructure to take responsibility for what she'd done. The enormity of that responsibility simply drove her mad. Because up to that point she had been blaming her husband. And seeing this was painful and really too much for her.

RH: What do you do to make that happen every night? That, in itself, is a big responsibility.

SC: You know, you just put one foot in front of the other. You start at the beginning and go through it each time. If you've done all your work and the performance is in place inside you, it's just a matter of doing it.

RH: What happens to that woman is painful to watch but also somewhat cathartic. It reminds me, though they are very different, of the woman in *Joe Egg*.

SC: Well, again we get back to those contradictions. I'd say there was a huge anger in Sheila. These people wouldn't believe this about her child. And the contradiction is that here is this warm, loving, wonderful woman who finally breaks through with this tremendous anger that's really been there all along. She's this absolute saint but, God, she's angry.

RH: You know, I find *Joe Egg* so difficult. I have two children and I have to ask myself, how would I deal with that? Sheila is really a brave woman.

SC: Yes, she is.

RH: I guess the anger makes her saintliness bearable.

SC: Yes, you're right.

RH: I want to ask this before we close: I'm asking everyone's feeling about this. Do you think there's a true place for critics, and if so, what is it?

SC: Well, I don't read notices myself.

RH: Do you read any notices?

SC: Well, I say I'm going to read them later, and then I don't. I guess I've read a few, and then friends call and leave them on your machine. I've heard them that way. And of course you get the gist of them from the way people act after opening—smiling or in a slump. At the time that they're relevant, you really can't read them, because, good or bad, you have to continue with what you're doing. And then, afterwards, it's like, who cares?

RH: Well, have we left anything out? I can't think of anything else at the moment.

SC: Well, I can't either.

RH: I appreciate this. Thank you so much.

SC: Well, thank you.

Photo by Emily Kuroda.

A Word Becomes a Life in Itself

SAB SHIMONO

This interview took place on Sunday, January 10, 1993, in a rehearsal room at the Mark Taper Forum in Los Angeles. Mr. Shimono was on a break from rehearsals for a new play *Fish Head Soup* by the Asian American playwright Philip Kan Gotanda. That seemed fitting because in recent years Mr. Shimono has become one of the premier interpreters of the words of Mr. Gotanda. Two of those roles—the father in *The Wash* and the older actor in *Yankee Dawg You Die*—are discussed here with Mr. Shimono's particular delight in detail and humor.

Roy Harris: When you read a script and decide that you want to do a part very much, what usually makes you feel that?

Sab Shimono: Actually, I always ask: does this character have a journey? And, what kind of journey is it? Because I'm Asian American, I look at whether I think it's written stereotypically. I ask if it's honest and if it comes from some sense of a real person. And I suppose (to be obvious), I consider the size of the role.

I'm also interested in style. For instance, I just did *Ninja Turtles III*, in which I play a Japanese war lord in the 1500s. I liked it because I liked the director, Stuart Gillard. The script was only so-so. At the auditions, he would make suggestions and I'd try them. I think, when I walked in, I wasn't what they had in mind. I try when I'm auditioning to bring to it what I think is really there, not what I think they might think. It's a risk, but I do it that way. And if the director accepts it and there's some vibration between us, we're in some good working condition. But if the director doesn't pick up at all on what I'm doing, we're in trouble. And, usually in that instance, I'd stay away from it.

RH: You mentioned a moment ago the character's *journey*. Is there any kind of journey that interests you more than another?

SS: Of course you want it to have lots of highs and lows. But really I've got to have humor. If it's not there, I find it. And if I can't find it, I will throw it in.

RH: Well, that's clear to me in all of your work. And particularly in the father in *Come See the Paradise*. In that very stern person was a sense of humor which made him real and, ultimately, moving.

SS: Well, you especially need it when the characters are basically heavy, as he was. I like humor, I think, partly because I like to entertain and to hear people laugh. I think it's boring when the actor just emotes out there.

RH: Let's say that now you've gotten a role and you know that in three weeks you'll begin rehearsal; what, if anything, do you do before rehearsals?

SS: Well, naturally I go over and over and over the script. But, actually, I think about the hair. I say, 'What kind of hair does this guy have? Is it long, short, curly, straight, combed, parted on one side or in the middle, smooth or jagged?' And when I find the hair (meanwhile, I'm looking at the character psychologically too), that starts the basis of my character.

For *Ninja Turtles III*, I thought, what can I do to make him different? Different was important here because they were going to make me a samurai, which means hair pulled back. But I thought he needed to look dangerous, and so I came up with the idea that his hair comes down one side of his face. And it worked, because in the fights it swings back and forth.

RH: Do you ever research a role?

136

SS: Well, working on the hair is a form of research. Sometimes I go to museums. When I did *Presumed Innocent*, for instance, I went to the coroner's office and, frankly, nearly fainted. I came to a real respect for coroners—to have to deal with that and then eat lunch. Sometimes, though, I don't feel it's that important to research. If you're playing a doctor, do you need to meet with one? Usually, what you will do as a doctor is already in the script, that's mapped out for you. But more important: what does he do after work? Or, if it's a character we see and know at home, what does he do at work? You need to research only what you are not already given. Research the unknown about your character.

"I go over and over and over the script. But, actually, I think about the hair. I say, 'What kind of hair does this guy have? Is it long, short, curly, straight, combed, parted on one side or in the middle, smooth or jagged?' And when I find the hair . . . that starts the basis of my character."

RH: Do you create a life away from the play for your character?

SS: If I'm in trouble I do, but not the whole play. Sometimes, it's just one line I can't get, and it's going nowhere so I'll build a story behind that line. And it may have nothing to do with the play. The most important thing for me is to juice myself by giving that line a life of its own. For my own form of research I really don't stick to the plot of the play.

RH: Is what you create about the line just for you?

SS: Yes. You're building a whole inner life that's just for you. It's why, in rehearsals, I ask a lot of questions but I don't give a lot of answers.

137

That's just for me. I hate, in rehearsal, to talk, talk, talk, talk. Too much talk can destroy something.

RH: Well, let's say, tomorrow in rehearsal you're going to work on Act I, scenes 1, 2, and 3. What sort of work would you do the night before?

SS: Well, first, I won't hold myself to learning the lines because it's the first day. I think you waste your time going to the first rehearsal thinking about what your lines are. I'd rather spend that time looking at the script—interpreting it—and come in with many questions. In fact, that's probably what I'd do, if anything. Have questions. I always have questions. People have said about me, "Sab doesn't say 'Good morning.' He asks a question."

RH: When you say *interpreting* the lines, what do you mean by that?

SS: Well, in terms of lines, it's: why does he say this when he might be saying something else? And the playwright or the director would give me his opinion about it. The most important thing to me is where your character falls in the whole scheme of the play. An actor is just one part of the whole. I have a tendency to get tunnel vision, and so I tell myself, look at the whole picture. Where does he fit in the whole?

In *The Wash* and *Yankee Dawg You Die*, both by Philip Gotanda, I was able to pace the show because I was always in it. In *Fish Head Soup*, Phil's current play I'm rehearsing, I can't pace it because my character is in a catatonic state. I'm not one of the drivers. The play is fragmented, it's monologue after monologue. It is fun to be the driving force because then the energy is there for two hours, and it never lets up. *Fish Head Soup* is very hard *because* the momentum comes and goes. That's why my homework has to be very thorough. And my impulses have to be very, very thorough.

RH: What is a good rehearsal situation? What do you like?

SS: A lot of laughter. People throwing out a lot of ideas without any censor. We are actually children when we rehearse, and we should be. We should be free to do whatever comes into our heads (without craziness, of course), anything exploratory. So the environment should be one of anything goes, with a lot of laughter.

138

Sab Shimono in the 1993 film *Ninja Turtles III*. Photo by Martha Cecilia.

RH: What are you looking for from other actors in a rehearsal situation?

SS: To listen. Because if they're not listening, they're by themselves. And you can't get anything. I love to get things from the other actors. I try always to listen.

RH: What is a rehearsal situation you remember with pleasure?

SS: In terms of rehearsals, I've been fortunate enough often to be one of the major characters. So I've been able to set the mood of the rehearsals. I have to say that mostly all my rehearsals have been pleasant.

RH: Have you ever had a situation that wasn't?

SS: Yes, when I was younger. We did a workshop and I was very good. Then we went into production, and all of a sudden this same director started *directing*. And he gave me all these strange directions that didn't make much sense. He started imposing things on me and screaming, and I got intimidated and couldn't do anything. And I learned from that experience that never again will a director intimidate me. I will come back or I will leave, but I will not be intimidated. It seems to me that if the director is bad, well, it's pretty hopeless.

RH: Since you mentioned this, and I was going to ask anyway, what do you want from a director?

SS: To leave me alone to do it. I don't mean leaving me alone and letting me go wild. He should be there to help. There's a tendency on the part of some directors that all of a sudden his direction is more important than your finding what's happening with this character; the direction becomes an ego trip. I also don't like directors who are two steps ahead of me in directions. I have to get it into my body. And anything intellectualized too early doesn't help me at all in the process. Maybe two days later I'll say to myself, 'Oh, I know what he means now.'

For me a good director is one who gives me some stimulus, some idea, not "Turn left," or "Turn right." Maybe two weeks later but not early on. Not "Sab, at this moment I want you to cry," or "At this moment speak faster." What they've become is, really, barriers, because the feeling is, "Oh, God, he told me to speak faster but I don't know why." Or, "I'm supposed to cry here. Why?" The worst thing a director can tell you is, "If you say the line right, you'll get a laugh."

RH: Well, sure, that ruins it for you.

SS: Of course. Let me discover that for myself. Leave me alone. Also, a good director is one who treats each actor differently because each actor is different. An actor must be treated with respect. You know, some actors need to be told, "Go here. Go there." I don't. At least not early on.

RH: Who's a director you've really liked working with?

SS: Sharon Ott. Oscar Eustis. Alberto Issac from East West Players. He gives you these ideas and you go home and think about it and come in

140

and show what you've done. He doesn't stage you, and ultimately what you have to do is stage it for yourself. And then, after a few weeks, he starts mapping it out. But the good thing is, I've already taken a journey on my own, so it's mine, and whatever he tells me to do I can do. We've done two plays together and it's worked both times.

RH: What did you like about Sharon Ott?

SS: She listened. We sat and talked about a line. Where does it come from? And she talked about her own experience—what happened with her own mother and father—and that made me think of a similar situation in my own family. And in this way the line comes alive for me. With Sharon, there's a lot of talking and listening rather than, "Okay, let's do the first scene. Okay, notes. You moved here—don't. Move there." We do get to that, but at the appropriate time. She can give you a very particular direction: "At this time put your glasses down and sigh," but only at the right time, when you're ready for it.

RH: Would you say that once you've done the appropriate groundwork you could do almost anything a director asked?

SS: Definitely.

RH: You mentioned earlier about hair being important to you. Do you ever get a picture of what the character should look like? or how he dresses?

SS: Once the hair comes in, everything else falls in place.

RH: How much does the costume you wear affect you?

SS: It affects me a lot. Usually I have some say in what it's going to be.

RH: Do you like to discuss with the designer?

SS: Oh, yes. I would never go against what a designer wanted—I respect what they are doing—but if it's very different from what I saw, I feel I have to voice that. But my mind can be changed.

RH: Have you had a costume that really worked for you?

141

SS: Well, in another Philip Gotanda play I did, a musical called *Avocado Kid*, I played a dodo bird. Actually, I made the whole costume myself out of anything I could find. I said, 'A dodo bird, he's a loser.' So I found this ostrich feather somewhere up in the attic at East West Players, and I cracked it, so it was always bent. And I wore these humongous slippers and white tights, and put towels and pillows in my butt. It worked for me.

RH: Have you ever had a costume that impeded you?

SS: Well, the play we discussed earlier. This was in the early '70s. I had to wear these shoes with very high heels and the stage was raked. The character was named Black Jack, and he was supposed to be an Asian guy who thinks black. So the director told me that black guys walk forward. But I had these heels on, on a raked stage yet, and he yelled, "Sab, you're not walking right." So, no, that costume did not work—high heels, raked stage, and a fake walk. Everything I'd worked on went out the window.

RH: I'm sure it did. How could it not? What's the longest run you've ever done of a drama? I know you did *Mame* for several years.

SS: The dramas I've done have always been limited runs. The longest would be *Yankee Dawg You Die*. I took it from Berkeley to Chicago to L.A. to New York.

RH: How do you keep something fresh that you've done often? Is there anything specific that you do?

SS: There are always moments in a play that aren't discovered. And if you try, during a performance, to crystallize one specific moment, that helps. You know, though, doing a play is such a privilege. After I've done it I'm so energized. It's great therapy to become another person. And it doesn't take much for me to do it once the audience is there.

RH: To somewhat shift the subject here: what do you see as the chief difference between acting on stage and acting for the camera?

SS: Well, in a play you have the responsibility of the whole for two hours. Whereas, when you work in a film you have to understand the whole, but for that day you concentrate on one particular scene. You

142

. . . with Stan Egi in the Playwrights Horizons production of Philip Kan Gotanda's *Yankee Dawg You Die*, 1990. Photo by Gerry Goodstein.

put all your focus into that one moment, and then you forget it and go on to the next moment. But in a play you have to think of the whole.

RH: You mention the word *whole*. When you do a film, most of the time you shoot out of context—the end first and then, maybe, the middle. Is that a problem for you?

SS: Yeah, it's a problem especially if you shoot the last first. Because later you always feel, "Oh, I wish I had done that." But what I've learned is, you've done it, it's over.

RH: What is a film experience that you really liked?

SS: I'd say the father in *Come See the Paradise*.

RH: What made you want to play him?

SS: The trouble he had when they placed him and his whole family in that Japanese internment camp in Colorado. It was a very juicy role. You know, I was surprised I got it.

RH: Why were you surprised?

SS: Because I thought I was too young for it. Actually, the most important thing to me about that project was that my family did go to camp. So doing that role was like being a part of film history. I thought a lot of my own father. Working with Alan Parker, the director, was a pleasure. He did his research, and he did bring life to that family. I was in camp myself.

RH: You must have been very young.

SS: I was three.

RH: Do you have memories of that that helped you with the role?

SS: Interesting you ask. I was probably the age of my grandchild in the film, Minnie. There's a scene where we're in the camp, and I make a chair for Minnie out of wood. Now, I have a twin brother. When we left camp in Colorado, we made a chair out of clay. And while I was shooting that scene, that memory came back to me. Very close to me, it was.

RH: Were you pleased with your work in the film?

SS: Basically. Alan Parker guided me and talked a lot about it, but basically he left me alone.

RH: When I watched it recently, I thought, why didn't this do better? It's very well made, beautiful to look at, and it's the kind of film Hollywood loves: an epic.

SS: Timing. That film came out in December two years ago, when we were in the midst of the war situation. It was not a hip, hip, hooray, America type of film. So when it came out, the studio pulled it very quickly.

RH: So far, is *Come See the Paradise* the best film experience you've had?

144

. . . in the 1990 film *Come See the Paradise*. Photo courtesy 20th Century Fox.

SS: In the grand scale I'd have to say, yes, because I developed such a close relationship with the family; we were together for a long time. *Presumed Innocent* was also very good, but it was only two days of shooting. It was interesting with *Come See the Paradise* because Alan Parker became part of the family. He is a director who becomes involved. When the camera's moving, he's one of the characters. Some directors are on the other side directing you, "Stand still. Move." Whereas, Alan becomes part of it—part of the wall, part of the furniture, part of a character in a scene with you. He's there.

RH: You mentioned *Presumed Innocent*. What was that like?

SS: I shot that—actually I didn't think I could do it—while I was shooting *Come See the Paradise*. So I was switching characters.

RH: How did you do it?

SS: The reason I could do it—and this is why I like movies better than television—was because I had both scripts about three months before shooting. So I had time to get ready. But it was crazy because I had to go to New York to shoot *Presumed Innocent*.

RH: Your character, the coroner, was fascinating because his evil was sort of ordinary. I have a particular question to ask you. When you're on the stand, and Harrison Ford is asking you all the questions, you used the word "sterile" and you pronounced it in an odd way. Do you remember what you did? You're looking at me now like, 'What? Is he crazy?' But it was as if the word had some special meaning for this coroner, and we got a glimpse of what it meant.

SS: I don't remember that specifically. But I do do that. For me a word becomes a life in itself. One word can sometimes give great richness and texture to a character.

RH: That coroner was on the side of something not so nice. Do you like playing characters who have an unpleasant edge to them?

SS: Not as such. But I get a lot of that kind of stuff. I like a character who's rich and complex.

RH: The father in *Come See the Paradise* has something sort of unpleasant about him—I guess *tough* is a better word. He's a bit of a dictator. But we feel for him, even before he gets to the camp and loses his dignity in that terrible way. Are you aware of those kinds of contradictions as you work on a role?

SS: Not consciously, but sometimes. There's a scene where I tell my daughter that she can't go out, and in the middle of my anger I took a moment that showed, I think, his hesitation about what he was saying. I like it where boom, boom, boom, you're angry, and then you have a tiny sparkle of something else. It deepens it, I think.

RH: Have you ever been ten minutes into a performance on stage and realized you were off in some way?

SS: Oh, yeah.

RH: What do you do to get yourself back?

SS: The first thing is once you realize it, just let it go. What helps me the most when this happens is to really listen to what's happening on

146

stage to get you back on track again. Also what helps is to physicalize something, and emotions will come from that. A lot of people say, "Well, how do you cry?" It's not so hard. If you do something physical to make yourself cry, that will also lead you to something emotional.

RH: Would you say that you work more from within or from without?

"For me a word becomes a life in itself. One word can sometimes give great richness and texture to a character . . . I like a character who's rich and complex."

SS: I work within but I rely on the handles from without. I can't always rely on my emotions, but I can rely on the physical gestures to help me get to them. If something doesn't feel right, I have to stop and ask the director to change things until it's right for me. Then maybe the director will say, "Do this," and by then, it's right for me because I've found something physical that will trigger it for me. I find triggers.

RH: Have you ever found a gesture or a movement that helped you understand the character as a whole better?

SS: Oh, yeah. The play I'm doing now: *Fish Head Soup*. He has a line, "I didn't want to see it, but I see it. The sickness. I see it everywhere." I didn't know what to do with it. Then all of a sudden, I did this gesture (as if I were keeping it from my eyes), and suddenly it opened up for me. Now all I have to do is the gesture, and it happens. Now I didn't plan this. I was just working and it happened.

RH: I find it fascinating how a gesture or a series of gestures can make a moment for a person.

SS: Oh, yeah. And sometimes the gesture can impede you. Like that director who wanted me to walk forward and I kept trying to do it, and it just didn't work. It never worked.

147

RH: Now I wanted to ask you, and I wrote myself a note earlier so I wouldn't forget: What made you want to do *Yankee Dawg You Die*?

SS: One thing, of course, was working with Philip Gotanda, and also I loved that character because he was so dashing in his white suit. The character itself was not me. I was actually more like the young boy who has dreams and gets angry at the older actor and asks, "Why did you take all these stereotypical roles?" In a way, playing someone who was so different from me was fascinating. As an actor, I had to justify why this character, an Asian American actor, would play *any* kind of role, no matter how stereotypical. Doing the role made me understand the actors of that generation and why they did those roles. Nothing else was available. They had to. And their sense of consciousness wasn't as great as ours. I think I really learned to appreciate their efforts.

RH: Will you go towards a play because of its subject even if, let's say, the character itself isn't so great?

SS: Yes, that's one of the reasons I did *Pacific Overtures*.

RH: Was that a good experience?

SS: It was a rich experience, yes. The thing I liked and found surprising was all this Asian American talent that Hal Prince got together that no one thought existed. And he made a major American musical out of it. (Then, fifteen years later, *Miss Saigon* happened, and people said, "There's no Asian American talent.") I was very proud to be a part of that production.

RH: What made you want to do *The Wash*?

SS: I first did the part of the lover in the movie, and then Philip asked me to play the father. I'd never played anything like that. It was fascinating finding that character. He too was so different from me. I think that's why I'd do any character now: because it's a challenge. Especially if it's not in my pocket. And that one wasn't. About three weeks into the run in New York, I still couldn't find it. Sharon Ott said to me, "Well, Sab, you wanted to play this part." And I said, "I didn't want to play it. Phil told me to play it." At that point I was still laying it out and not ready

148

. . . with Nobu McCarthy in the Manhattan Theatre Club production of Philip Kan Gotanda's *The Wash*, 1988–89 season. Photo by Gerry Goodstein.

to push. And then something clicked. My instinct went into full gear, and it came out.

RH: Do you remember when it clicked?

SS: I know it was in the third week. It started to click when the hair worked. This one I was fighting. I thought his hair should be long. And it got shorter and shorter and shorter, until it was very close to the skin. And that worked.

RH: In what way did it work?

SS: I looked at the face and said, 'That's a tough-looking face.' And the cropped hair made it look tougher. It was also virile and exposed. And then everybody in the play touched my head. They almost caressed this stubby head. And the more they caressed me, the meaner I got.

RH: Did you prefer playing one over the other?

SS: I liked them both. They were so different. I would have to say I liked playing the father a little better because he was a completely new character for me. At first, you see, I didn't think the father had humor. Each character has his own humor and finding that always leads me to who the person is. Also, I'd say, in playing the father the voice became important.

RH: In what way?

SS: Well, lower, *down there*, more guttural. Grumbly. I had to find the right placement for the voice. Actually, I don't go search for it. Voice becomes instinct, too. Sometimes the voice will just go *down there* while you're working on it; sometimes it just goes *up there*.

RH: If you could work with any actor in the business now, who would it be?

SS: Well, I would really like to work with Bob DeNiro. We studied together with Stella Adler. I remember looking into his eyes even then, and it was all there. Everything you needed was there. We started out together and we're at this point in our careers, and it just doesn't feel complete yet. He's very important to me because he's part of my beginning. Actually, from our class, he and I are the only ones still acting (at least as far as I know). I'd like to make that circle complete now by working with him.

RH: You know, this has been fascinating. Everyone is so different, everyone has his own way of approaching this.

150

SS: In the past, you know, roles for Asian actors have been very limited. I've been very fortunate because in the last twenty years there have come to be a number of good Asian American playwrights and I've had the opportunity to work with most of them. And that means I've been able to play who I am from my own background. As a pioneer, I've been able to explore a new aspect of our culture. I have made myself available to many Asian American projects over the years, and I will continue to do so because I feel I'm their instrument.

Photo by Beverly Hall.

A Good Intimacy of Feeling

CYNTHIA NIXON

Cynthia Nixon is the actress about whom Bob Leonard said in his interview: "She's like a dancer. . . . Something happens when that actress walks on stage. It elevates into another world." She brings to everything she does a clearheaded insight and a passionate maturity far beyond her twenty-six years. This interview took place on Friday, November 20, 1992, in a rehearsal room next door to the Mitzi Newhouse Theater at Lincoln Center. Miss Nixon had just opened in the lead role of Eleanor Ames in Neal Bell's *On the Bum* at Playwrights Horizons.

Roy Harris: When you decide to do a role, what makes you want to do it?

Cynthia Nixon: You know, I've changed my mind about that recently. Because I've done several leads in a row now, I'm asking myself, 'Does that mean you only do leads? Do you take smaller roles because it's on Broadway and pays well? how do you decide? what's your criterion?' There's a lot of satisfaction in doing roles that carry a play, but you can't always expect that.

So I've decided to try to start looking for characters that I've never played. This has never really been a consideration before. I was reading a script the other night, and there were a lot of women's parts that were in my age range, and I decided that if I was going to audition, I'd audition for this one role because it was really unusual—something people didn't associate with me.

Actually, I think the play probably comes first in my consideration of what role to play. You know, my first question is often, do I love the play?

RH: Well, I was going to ask you anyway, since I've just seen it and you were so fine, what made you want to play Eleanor Ames in *On the Bum*?

CN: Well, I was astonished by Neal Bell's script when I first read it. My connection was to the play itself and not to the character. In fact, I had a lot of trouble finding the character—I'm still having trouble. But the play seemed to be saying something so important. There are very few plays I've read that have the scope of *On the Bum*.

RH: You were talking a moment ago about lead roles and supporting roles, and Eleanor Ames is a lead. In *The Heidi Chronicles*, you played two supporting roles, Becky in Act I and Denise in Act II. What made you want to do that play?

CN: There were several reasons. First, I hadn't been on Broadway in a while. Then, I had been a huge fan of Wendy's because I had seen *Isn't It Romantic* at Marymount when I was a kid. It had such an impact. Also, I have such a warm feeling about Playwrights Horizons, and the idea of working with the people there was pleasing. So, really it was more about the play and the situation than about the roles themselves.

RH: When you get a role, what sort of work do you do before you get into rehearsal?

CN: I do very little, almost nothing, other than read it. However, when I did *Romeo and Juliet* at the Public, that was different. I had never done any Shakespeare. I had never had any training for it, but I had been working on the role on my own for eight years or so. So, when I went into rehearsal I already knew the lines.

RH: Do you ever research a role?

CN: I have. But I don't know whether it's ever paid off particularly. I did a show years ago about the Civil War, and we had a lot of time to prepare for it. The whole company had meetings with a vocal coach and worked on accents. I kept my radio tuned to the country-western radio stations. I read *Gone with the Wind*.

154

Cynthia Nixon with Campbell Scott in Neal Bell's *On the Bum*, Playwrights Horizons, 1992. Photo by Joan Marcus.

RH: Wouldn't you say that was research?

CN: Oh yeah. You know, when I go into rehearsal and there's a dramaturg around who has information about the playwright or about the period or what different people have written about the character, I always have fun reading it. But I don't know if I've ever done research that I felt really helped me. Or maybe it did unconsciously.

RH: Okay, let's say you've had the first day of rehearsal. The company has read through the play. Tomorrow you're going to rehearse Act I, scenes 1, 2, 3. Do you do any homework beforehand, of any kind?

CN: Yeah, I sit with the script and try and break it down, not so much into beats, but into 'In these four lines, what are they really talking about? What is the playwright trying to do here?' In a very good play,

155

you do have to dig for it because it's not readily apparent on the surface. So I look for what it all means.

RH: When you're in the rehearsal process what are you looking for from other actors?

CN: You know, people are so different, have such different ways of working. It can be the opposite of mine and often it's fine. You can have an actor who sits and talks with you about the scene and what you're both trying to achieve, and you create a whole history together.

RH: Do you like to talk it all out?

CN: I like to just because I like to talk. But I really think the better way to go is each actor clinging very tightly to his own character and trying to be very sure of what they're doing. So much of theatre is about conflict, for two actors to get together and decide exactly what that conflict is, could take away from the conflict. That way of working is less effective than if you just let it happen and let the director figure it all out.

Actually, some of the best work I've done was with actors with whom I had very little relationship off stage. Of course, there are certain relationships in a play, like good friends, or mother and daughter, where a lot of knowledge helps. And, too, if the characters have had a big past together, it helps to get some of that clear.

RH: You said something that made me think of the relation of you and Campbell Scott in *On the Bum*, partly because it's so mysterious. He steps on the stage . . .

CN: And the whole play changes, I know.

RH: Well, there's a huge sense of unspoken conflict. Did you and he talk a lot?

CN: No, we didn't. Things just happened. He's a very sweet person, but very private, and very much in his own head, I think. That may account for some of the mysterious feeling you got.

RH: The relation of you and that character was so fascinating that I wanted more of it as I watched the play.

156

. . . with Anne Lange, Joanne Camp, Joan Allen, and Ellen Parker in the Broadway production of Wendy Wasserstein's *The Heidi Chronicles*, Plymouth Theatre, 1989. Photo by Peter Cunningham.

CN: A lot of people have felt that.

RH: It's almost a chemical reaction to each other, and knowing I was going to talk to you, it made me wonder, how much of it was consciously worked out?

CN: Well, that chemical thing is what you want. It's really a connection and a not-connection at the same time.

RH: Would you say that you are more a planned sort of actress, or more spontaneous and intuitive?

CN: I don't know how to answer that. I guess I actually think I'm planned. This is a hard one. I know I definitely work from my head, and I don't necessarily—particularly when we're in an exploratory stage in rehearsal—plan what the moment is going to be. But I definitely come into rehearsal with an agenda.

RH: You may not know fully how you work. That's all right. I want your view of it at this moment.

CN: It's very hard to know whether to define it as intuitive or planned. I always have a very definite external color of the scene, or view of the scene. And sometimes I become inarticulate about it when the director

157

is trying to get me to do something completely different. I don't know if that's intuitive or planned.

RH: Well, a good actor is both. I ask the question because I'm interested in how you see yourself.

CN: I guess I'd have to say I'm really more instinctive.

RH: What irritates you the most about another actor's way of working in rehearsal?

CN: Actors who are afraid. It makes me very angry—those people who are afraid of embarrassing themselves, afraid of not being good, afraid of getting into a scene and becoming lost, or are scared of whatever emotions the scene brings up. And, so, they find ways of stonewalling the process.

RH: How has this happened?

CN: For instance, they sit around and talk forever and refuse to ever let you get up on your feet. They talk about what's wrong with the scene. Now, that's perfectly legitimate as a means of getting to your feet, but to do it to stall, no. Also, there's the actor who steps way back from the play and talks about "the themes of the play" because there's something they're avoiding. It's fine to do that, but too often it's a real trap.

RH: What's a good relation you had with an actor on stage, an instance of where it really worked for you?

CN: Oh, that's hard.

RH: You can say, "I don't know," or "God, don't ask such a stupid question."

CN: I had a really good time with Lisa Gay Hamilton. We worked together in *Servy 'n Bernice*. Terry Kinney directed it, and the style in which it was directed was improvisatory. You know, some nights a moment would be very angry and then the next night it might be silly or sad. So it was partly the framework that Terry had given us, a certain freedom. The two characters were best friends, and we were becoming friends off stage. So both of those things allowed for a good intimacy of feeling.

RH: What other actors have you liked working with?

158

. . . with Christine Baranski and Jeremy Irons in *The Real Thing*, Plymouth Theatre, 1984. Photo by Martha Swope.

CN: Well, Jeremy Irons was amazing in *The Real Thing*.

RH: What made him amazing?

CN: His facility. Even now I see him in things, and he is as stunning as he was in our play. With most actors I can see what they're doing. It's probably a British/American thing. He's of a different species. I don't understand what he's doing and what he's trying to do and how he does what he does. He's so fascinating and he conveys such depth. He defines the character so well, and it was him and it wasn't him. I think it must really be subtext; I think it has to do with the fact that he doesn't, unlike

159

myself, feel he has to get all this stuff forward. He's so internalized, while at the same time he's not small. I see him in things, and he's so different from one thing to another. It's not like a Meryl Streep, a transformative kind of thing. He's so internal.

RH: Around the same time, you were working with William Hurt in *Hurlyburly*.

CN: He's the opposite of what I said before about actors who are afraid and stave off. He's very courageous. He would just charge in fearlessly and thrash around and try many different things. I would have my last scene with him every night, and he had just gone through this tremendous crushing play—it was like *Lear* for that character. And he didn't seem to have any particular obligation about where he had to get, so sometimes the last moments of the play would be very angry or sometimes numb or sometimes hurt. It was an experience to work with him each night.

RH: What are you most looking for from a director?

CN: The thing I'm most looking for—and I'm surprised to realize this as I say it now—is someone who has a point of view. Someone who knows what he or she wants, even if I disagree with it. And sometimes directors don't know, and that's okay. And if they don't know, they say so, and eventually you come to a place (hopefully) where you don't need help anymore or a place where they'll be able to help you again.

But it's the most frustrating thing in the world to have a director who doesn't have any ideas, and doesn't know what he thinks when he sees what you're doing. So you keep trying things and you look out there for some feedback, and it's like nobody's there. You do a scene two very different ways, and they don't know or they're afraid to choose.

I've worked with a lot of directors that I've really, really loved, and I would say that, almost, my favorite director I've worked with—and he wasn't a stage director—was Milos Forman in the film *Amadeus*.

RH: Why was he a favorite?

CN: I've never had anyone who had that exact an idea of what he wanted. He directed me ad infinitum in the auditions for *Amadeus*. He would read the scenes with me as the other actor. He would stop me

160

. . . with William Hurt in David Rabe's *Hurlyburly*, Barrymore Theatre, 1984. Photo by Martha Swope.

every few sentences and give specific notes. He was so precise about what he wanted, and it was so helpful.

RH: It must be helpful, particularly in film where things happen in such an odd, disjointed way.

CN: Oh, back to your question about instinctual or planned. Let me say this: I start from an instinctual place, but then by the time we get into it, I get very planned and precise. Partly, I think it comes from being a kid actor, and having my mother for so many years as the person with whom I rehearsed at home. She was the person I bounced ideas off of. I was trying to get straight in my mind what I wanted to do. Because my mother and I could spend as much time as we wanted, we would go moment by moment. Of course, it's very rare to be able to get a director to spend that kind of time with you. So I really like that kind of precise, going over every detail.

RH: It's interesting that you mention Milos Forman because there's an image of you in that film I've never forgotten. It was before I was well

161

acquainted with your work. It's an image of you pushing open a door and looking.

CN: Yeah, I know where you mean.

RH: I'll never forget that picture of you. It's interesting that I remember it because you're not in the final version of the film so much.

CN: And I wasn't in it very much from the beginning. They didn't cut anything. He spent all that detailed time with me on such a really insignificant part.

RH: Now you worked twice with Mike Nichols and both in the same season. Very few actors have had that kind of experience. You did, if I remember, Act I and III of *Hurlyburly* at the Barrymore and in between you'd run to the Plymouth to play Jeremy Irons's daughter in *The Real Thing*. What was that like?

CN: Well, it's really like doing both Becky and Denise in *The Heidi Chronicles*.

RH: But you were running from theatre to theatre. What was that like?

CN: It wasn't quite as formidable as it may sound. First, I did *The Real Thing*. We had a leisurely rehearsal period, went to Boston, brought it back to Broadway. I had been playing it for several months when we went into rehearsal with *Hurlyburly*. I left *The Real Thing* and we took *Hurlyburly* to Chicago for six weeks, then to the Promenade off-Broadway and finally to Broadway. Our moving it to Broadway happened to coincide with the woman who replaced me in *The Real Thing* leaving the show for a movie. And the part opened up again, and it was something Mike and I had joked about. So I said, "Well, you know, I can do it," and he said, "Sure, let's try it." It helped enormously that I had done each of them separately first. So all the onstage relationships were set up, and I had relationships with all the actors. In effect, it really was like doing two different roles in the same play. I was able to take both curtain calls.

RH: Well, fascinating. You've had a chance to work with some really wonderful directors. What is Mike Nichols like to work with?

162

CN: He's also one of the best directors I've ever worked with. You know, so often a director is like a teacher. There's such a cult of personality that springs up about them that you want to come to class and you want to do well, and you want to please them and impress them. And he's one of those people. Even forgetting about all of the amazing things he's done in film and on stage, he's just a funny, clever, and wise person. The anecdotes that he spins are smart, and he uses them to illustrate his points. He can weave such a magic spell around the whole experience.

RH: Is he a director who allows you to find your way or is he more of a guide?

CN: It's been a while since I worked with him but my main memories are that first, he sets the stage. He talks about particular issues, tones that we'd like to strike. You kind of meander for a while, and then at a certain point he comes up to you, or at least he came up to me and said, "You're not getting it; it's not there. Where is it?" And of course, you find it. And then the great thing—and it spoils you for almost any other director—he felt you have to get *everything* absolutely right.

RH: So he's scrupulous?

CN: The amount of time he would take over every detail: the acting, of course; but the set; the transitions between scenes; the particular pair of shoes you're wearing; the little thing on the table downstage right. I'm that kind of person myself about details. It's so important to me: the play's being complete.

RH: What's the worst situation you've had with a director? I'm asking the question because I'm interested in why it wasn't good from an actor's point of view.

CN: Well, I've had two really bad experiences. One was a director who hadn't really done a lot of directing yet, and knew what he liked when he saw it, but had very little experience knowing what goes into making something work from inside. So we went right up on our feet. We barely read it, almost no discussion. And he was so interested in *setting* it that we had the play blocked in two days. And, of course, we didn't take it apart. And he just kept running it and running it. I would try to talk to him about why a particular scene wasn't working, what was happening in the scene and why that wasn't happening in what we were doing. And it would almost be like he hadn't read the play. His experience had been so much as a viewer. If something worked, for instance, once in a rehearsal, he'd say, "Oh, that was great, when you touched his hair like that." And he didn't understand that it wasn't the fact that I touched his hair, it was *why* I had touched his hair, my motive. But he would get so excited over outward stuff, that that's what he'd go after.

RH: How much are you affected by externals? Do you ever get a picture in your mind of what the character should look like, or how she should dress?

CN: Sometimes I do. Externals have such a big impact on the audience. I don't remember ever having a costume that impeded what I was doing; I know some actors have. Well, you know though, when you've been doing a role for a long time and you really can't imagine doing it without *those* shoes. You become melded to them and they become a part of you. To do it without them is unthinkable.

RH: You wear a pale green blouse in *On the Bum*. I don't know what it is about it, but it struck me because of the way it hangs on your body.

CN: It is a wonderful blouse. When Sharon Lynch, our designer, showed me things that she wanted to use, I knew immediately which ones I wanted, and luckily, they were the ones Don Scardino wanted. They both felt that that blouse, while certainly of the period, reminded them of my own clothes.

RH: So that costume helps you?

CN: Definitely. I felt really comfortable. One thing about all the costumes in the show is that they are from the period. And that helps give you a feel for the time you're in. If we had a very long run, they'd have to be replaced because they're falling apart. The authenticity is something. Well, the look of the whole shows helps us do it every night.

RH: It's also done with such taste, with Don's great simplicity of approach. For instance, I usually hate sex on stage, but you and Campbell Scott in that beautiful tableau that lets us know what happened without

164

being explicit. And because it's not, it is sexy. The two of you have such a strong chemistry that it was simply a moment of incredible connection.

CN: You know, it's so funny about that scene because everyone I know who's seen the show mentions it, and it didn't seem to be a majorly sexual scene at all.

"There's a stride you hit on stage; as the evening goes on you get better and better. But that's really true with film because the farther along you get in shooting, the better you get. I certainly do. One thing that's so important in film is to not lose your momentum."

RH: It wasn't, and that's why it works. What is the worst moment you ever had on stage?

CN: I've had a lot of terrible moments. Once I was doing *The Master Builder* at Hartford Stage, and Sam Waterston and I were involved in this very passionate . . . not really love scene, but passionate anyway. And in the middle of it, I farted. The audience didn't hear it but he did. Our eyes just locked, and I didn't even say my next line. It just stopped me dead.

I had another moment in the same production where he and I were walking around with our eyes locked in this very intense death-life struggle, and he says, "Sit down. I must tell you something." We'd had a two-show day and I was really tired and I started to sit and there was no chair there. I reached back and sat down very slowly thinking that I would find the chair. I didn't. There are others, too.

RH: To change the subject somewhat, what do you see as the chief difference in acting for the stage and acting for the camera?

CN: Well, I've been doing so much theatre of late that I've gotten far away from film.

165

RH: Do you like doing film?

CN: Well, in the abstract I do. I've had a fair amount of film experiences that have been good. But I find I'm somewhat leery of it. To me, a play is wonderful because you have a group of people who do it with you every night. You huddle together, you work things out, it's like an acrobatic team. You know you can depend on each other, you're there for each other.

Now, in film, it's so fractured and disjointed. You're so alone. It's you and the camera. And if you're doing a role with enough stuff to it, you shoot for a long time, and gradually you find that relationship between you and the camera. What's scary about film is that you have to start from a place that hasn't been collectively explored.

RH: What role have you liked playing in film?

CN: I did an after school special called "It's No Crush, I'm in Love" when I was about eighteen. I played the main character, so I was in every scene. There's a stride you hit on stage; as the evening goes on you get better and better. But that's really true with film because the farther along you get in shooting, the better you get. I certainly do. One thing that's so important in film is to not lose your momentum. In this after school special, I was in every setup. So the whole machinery just kept moving.

RH: When you shoot something out of sequence, how do you work that out in your mind? Or do you do anything consciously with it?

CN: Shooting out of sequence is very difficult, and you can make yourself absolutely nuts with it. For instance, if you're on a two-month shoot, and you find your character two weeks into it, and there's all this stuff you've already shot, it's terrible. The best you can hope for is you have some rehearsal and you work it out in rehearsal, and that you have a director with a very strong eye and other actors that you work well with. It's really like a bunch of shapes that you have to get in the right place. And you lay down one shape, and then another shape, and then a third shape. And then you think, "Oh, I've done it wrong." But it's too late. So you have to say, "Well, these three shapes being what they are, what's the best I can do?"

166

RH: What do you see as your most successful role in film?

CN: With the exception of the first courtroom scene, I like the work I did in a miniseries called *The Murder of Mary Phagan.*

RH: I was planning to ask you about that; it's good and all the acting is very fine. What made you want to do that role?

CN: I didn't really want to do it. My agent sent me in. It was an interesting situation. The director who had been involved with the script for many years didn't have much knowledge of New York actors. So he let the casting director Howard Feuer pick mostly anyone he wanted. They brought me in for this role, and I think I read for it—I might have just talked to them. And they offered it to me, and I thought, 'Well, I don't know if I want to do it. It's not very large.' And then my agent who had been very patient finally said, "Do the role. You need to earn some money and it's a prestigious project." So I did it. And the baffling thing is I have no idea why I like my work there. It looks good to me, but I don't know why.

RH: Well, the character is really an unlikable person. She lies, and she's one of the chief reasons he's convicted. But you get a sense of her inner turmoil when she's testifying, and oddly we feel for her.

CN: Well, maybe it was two things. It was the nature of how fine the script was—there was just endless amounts of subtext there—and the other thing was the actors I was working with. The level of the acting, the calibre of it was incredible. Peter Gallagher, W.H. Macy, Paul Dooley, Kevin Spacey, and Jack Lemmon, among many others.

RH: What was Jack Lemmon like to work with?

CN: He was so protective of the actors, and he was very good to me. I had one long scene with him. The director and I had some disagreement about how a particular scene should be played. Jack understood the situation and he said to me, "You keep doing what you were doing in rehearsal. It's just perfect."

RH: You said you'd do the first courtroom scene differently. What would you do differently?

CN: Everything else I did in that role was so clear. You could see her mind working, and I think because that scene was about being molested, well, I was embarrassed by it. I just didn't really explore the scene. I think I kept it at arm's length. And so, I'd explore that more fully now.

RH: To change the subject again, do you think there's a true place for criticism in the theatre?

CN: Oh, absolutely. I definitely do.

RH: Has a critic ever said anything about your work that had you understand yourself better?

CN: Yes. I think that's one reason why they're important. I don't read reviews until we're closed. After *The Master Builder* closed, I read all the reviews, and they were very positive. But they did have a fair amount to say about my voice, and particularly in the third act of the play. It was "high pitched" and "out of control" and "difficult to listen to." And it was helpful to me to realize that. When you're dealing with emotions that are so huge, you feel, 'Anything I can do to get to that pitched feeling is justified.' I value what was said about my voice there. It made me look for deeper ways to get the feeling I want.

RH: What's your favorite role on stage?

CN: I really liked doing Honey in *Who's Afraid of Virginia Wolfe?* First, it was such fun to be on stage with Glenda Jackson, John Lithgow, and Brian Kerwin. I feel that of all the characters I've played that I really got that one and maybe even took it to a new plane. I hope so. Many people have said that they love my work in *On the Bum*, and I'm very glad, but I'm surprised. As much as I've enjoyed doing it, I feel I don't have the character yet.

RH: Maybe that's why it's so good. It's constantly evolving.

CN: Well, maybe. I'm a logical person and I like to pin everything down, and with this one I can't seem to do that. This is a role that I truly don't understand and that gave me problems along the way. But I just sort of go with it even though I don't understand it.

RH: What was your biggest problem with it?

168

CN: I had a lot of trouble trying to balance Eleanor's naiveté, her innocence, her not knowing anything and being open to everything, with that been-around-the-block, hard-bitten, smart-talking quality. I wrestled with it for a long time and it's a very important part of the character, that smart-talking aspect. Don kept pressing that as an issue. Sometimes I would think, 'Oh, he's right, it's in the character and I have to do it.' And sometimes I'd think, 'It's just not there.' This is a difficult play for the audience, and if they don't have a completely sympathetic person to follow, it's hard for them. But trying to find the balance between those two hasn't been easy, and I'm still working on it.

Photo by Kate Rettino.

A Sense of Community

ROGER REES

This interview took place on Wednesday, May 13, 1992, in the stage manager's office of the Mitzi E. Newhouse Theater at Lincoln Center. Mr. Rees was performing in Jon Robin Baitz's *The End of the Day* at Playwrights Horizons, for which he won an Obie Award a month later. One of the reasons that I wanted to interview Roger Rees, along with the fact that he is a wonderfully gifted and versatile actor, is that his background and training are very different from most of the other actors here. He was an Associate Artist of the Royal Shakespeare Company for over twenty years. That is a form of training largely unavailable to American actors. Does it make his way of working appreciably different?

Roy Harris: When you read a play and decide that you want to do a role, what makes you feel that?

Roger Rees: Well, I suppose if you had a kind of overview of someone's career, you'd probably notice a pattern, that they were attracted to certain kinds of roles. But it's a little different with me. I depend on a sense of anticipation, actually—a sense of what I might be able to give the world if I take the part. Or I may find I am more interested in the project than in what I myself get to say. When I'm encouraged by the author, or director, or artistic director, or a fellow actor to do a play, and as a result I get a sense that this might be a good play or an important play to participate in, I frequently say yes without reading the script. Of course, when one is working with companies of excellent people, that helps you be more dangerous, perhaps, in your choices.

Alternatively, if I feel it's a piece of rubbish, I count my lines and scenes, and if there are enough of 'em, I say "sure." Just a joke.

RH: Well, you're now doing Robbie Baitz's *The End of the Day*. Would the fact that it was a particular playwright affect your choice to do a play?

RR: Yes, of course. Anthony Hopkins once said to me that he doesn't read a script until he knows who's going to direct it. It's actually very difficult for an actor—if you have any sort of complexity about you—to assess what you might do with a role just by reading a script. That's why sometimes it's good to be advised by other people who've seen your work, or who have worked with the playwright or director, and to accept a role based in part on recommendation and trust.

RH: Everyone is different in the way they make choices about what to do. Julie Harris said she must feel an emotional connection to a character. Stockard Channing said she's got to hear it out loud, to see what's going on between the people. The variety of takes on this is interesting to me.

RR: I think, in the end, I believe that I am a rather anonymous entity, and that I can fashion out of this anonymity just the sort of man the script wants. Though in rehearsals, I may suddenly get alarmed because I'll see that the script wants something I had no idea it wanted. That can be scary.

RH: Once you've decided to do a role, do you do any preparation before rehearsals?

RR: The truth?

RH: Sure.

RR: No.

RH: Other than read it?

RR: Not even read it.

RH: Really?

Roger Rees with Nancy Marchand in Jon Robin Baitz' *The End of the Day*, Playwrights Horizons, 1992. Photo by T. Charles Erickson.

RR: No. Oh, I might look through it the night before the first read-through, to look up any long words that might be embarrassing for me if I didn't know how to pronounce them.

RH: But if you knew, for example, that you were going to have to do a Scottish (or a Hungarian) accent, would you work on that?

RR: Well, a lot of accents come easily to me. But I suppose if it were a particular American accent, I'd have to get some help. Even then, though, I'd wait until the rehearsals had started. I'm always anxious to keep all my options open. No decisions before rehearsals for me. Nancy Marchand puts it very nicely. When people ask her, "How is the play going?" she says, even on the last day, "It's too soon to tell." Life is more interesting to me than any one play. Let's study that. Then when you start to work on the play, there's a base to start from. For example, at the Royal Court I once was playing a zoologist who specialized in extinct

173

species. Before rehearsals, I became a vegetarian because I figured this fellow wouldn't want to help make any species extinct. That was seven years ago. I'm still a vegetarian.

RH: Okay. You're in rehearsal, and tomorrow you're going to work on the first two scenes of the play. Do you do any sort of work the night before? Any homework?

RR: I think that no matter how much you know about what your character may do before he enters, no one in the audience will. I use myself to fashion a character out of the words and the pauses and the action of the play. So I don't do much homework beyond saying the words many times over. On the other hand, if I were playing a trapeze artist or a ballet star or someone who sets himself on fire every night and jumps into a glass of water, I suppose I'd be busy doing research.

RH: Do you ever get a mental picture of what the character should look like?

RR: I don't know. If you told me I were going to play Romeo, I would see myself climbing up to the balcony, panting for breath. If you told me I were going to play Juliet, I would see myself leaning over the balcony, with long golden tresses full of flowers. Everything after that is downhill.

RH: What do you mean?

RR: Every experience in the rehearsal room, in the theatre too, is less, somehow, than what you first envisage.

RH: Well, that's how life is very often.

RR: That's why I try to envisage as little as possible before rehearsals. It's less of a disappointment when you come face to face with the reality. And then, in rehearsal, I just sort of like to go apeshit. I drag in a lot of embarrassment, and the good thing about that is that the options are left wide open.

RH: When you're in rehearsal, what are you looking for from other actors?

RR: A sense of community. A sense that everyone is part of the team, and there's an equality, right down to the janitor who might be passing

174

through and yells out, "I don't understand that." I don't care for people who have too grand an idea of themselves. And I don't like when people get to a sense of perfectness. If there were a perfect way to do a play, we wouldn't need a theatre. Each play would be done once, perfectly, and we'd all be off doing something else with our lives.

"They say you can't play King Lear; everyone around you plays it for you. I don't think any good play is necessarily about any one person's performance. It's the sense of community amongst the people doing it."

RH: What's an example of a good situation you've been in with actors?

RR: Well, many times with the RSC, because there was always a strong sense of common purpose. I had very happy times there because the community was such a strong one, so tightly knit. We did a production of *The Suicide*. In New York, there was a big Broadway production with Derek Jacobi. But the play is really a circus farce from Russia in 1926. It was a major role for me, and what made me good was that everyone around me was remarkable. They say you can't play King Lear; everyone around you plays it for you. I don't think any good play is necessarily about any one person's performance. It's the sense of community amongst the people doing it.

RH: It's interesting that you mention this. A week ago, in preparation for this talk with you, I watched the whole tape of *Nicholas Nickleby*, and it has the strongest sense of community I've ever seen. Was that truly a great experience?

RR: Oh, sure.

RH: How did it happen? Did you know the adaptation and say, "I want to do this?"

RR: We were doing a major season of Shakespeare and some Russian plays. There were fifteen of them being performed continuously. And everyone in the company was in every play. The nucleus of the group had been together for a long time. This was about 1979, and we'd been working intimately together since 1976. One thing I'd like to add about *community* is that it doesn't mean subservience. *Nickleby* was populated by many extremely vain actors, contesting vigorously for parts. Within that was an amity, a concern, a care. But there was also *demand*. Aggression is a positive thing.

RH: One of the things you feel about *Nickleby* is that everyone is so good that they demand that everyone else be equally good.

RR: That's right.

RH: It was extraordinary to see. You use the word *aggression*; that's certainly there.

RR: And in that experience, the director had no more right to talk about a performance than did anyone else. Everything was discussed, everything. It's the only way to preserve the organic functioning of the play.

Anyway, we were in the midst of this large season of many diverse works. Once we'd got the season on, the British government insisted that, because so much of what we'd done had an improvisational feel, we didn't need very much money to keep doing it. Therefore, we would have to manage by closing down the London end of the company and working only at Stratford. Well, we found this unacceptable, so we had to find a piece of work that would cost nothing, have no royalties, no scenery, no costumes. And we'd use everyone in it. And someone suggested that we do a Dickens piece. And we got interested in one, and I can't remember which one it was now. But that didn't work out. Then came *Nicholas Nickleby*. And it's a pretty tripey old book really, full of waywardness and a meandering forgetfulness. It goes on far too long. I'm sure many people said that about our play.

RH: Dickens did write it in episodes to be published in a magazine.

RR: Yeah, well, there are some characters that are left high and dry. And some things in the book are really just not ended. But all in all, what George Orwell said about Dickens is true. There is "this generous anger," which seemed to suggest that the play would have some political

. . . with Priscilla Morgan and Emily Richard in the Royal Shakespeare Company's production of *The Life and Adventures of Nicholas Nickleby*, Plymouth Theatre, 1982. Photo by Martha Swope.

value. So, we started to work on it. And this was back before David Edgar came in. We were just doing the work ourselves. Some fifty people. Actually, I smashed myself up in my car the night before the first day, so I wasn't even there.

In the process, several of us were given specific chapters to work on, because the book is eight hundred pages long. Everyone researched. Some people studied the drama of the period, how it was done. Others researched the postal system in London at that time. Everything that could be studied from the period was presented. Sometimes very amusingly. For instance, someone gave a lecture as if he were the man who ran the sewage works in Battersea. And the people who researched opera presented a little opera. And the people who researched clothes found items to show us. It was extraordinary—and very comprehensive. But really, it was all actually a way of massaging the material into some kind of workable shape, some sort of three dimensional piece.

RH: This sort of process is very rare as far as I know.

RR: Well, we were continuously improvising on the text, trying to find ways to create a drama out of what was essentially a narrative, looking for the emotional thrust. And it was much more difficult than we imagined, because the prose is so florid and abandoned and runs on so much.

RH: Well, Dickens has a way of telling the story through the description, and that's really not possible in the theatre.

RR: No, of course not.

RH: The wonderful thing about the piece is that it seems so true to what Dickens was after, and the human conflicts are so richly there. One of the things that struck me was the relation of Nicholas and Smike. It was tremendously moving. But there aren't any scenes where you watch it develop. How do you make something like that happen, where there isn't a build-up in the text itself?

RR: You bring up an interesting thing. A lot of theatre, you know, works by default, by what's not there, and by what you make the audience create in its mind. There was almost no set: a wagon and a few sticks of furniture, no costumes to speak of. What's glorious about all this is that you now can release your imagination. The audience is free, too. So if they see two characters like Smike and Nicholas catch a look across a stage, it says much more than many words can do.

RH: Of course.

RR: So, I would say that the friendship between Nicholas and Smike provided a place for the audience to put their need for that kind of friendship, their desire for it.

RH: Well, at the end of the first evening, you and Smike are leaving Dotheboys Hall. You say something like, "I'm going home," and Smike

178

looks at you and says, "You are my home." It was hugely moving. The story has a built-in drama of need that's classic, and we all respond to that. As you said, who doesn't need?

RR: That's right. Dickens proved that popular art is in the imagination. Certainly Shakespeare proved it, too. And *Nicholas Nickleby* required the audience to use its imagination.

RH: Another thing that struck me was that the language didn't seem stilted at all. It felt like how we talk. When you work on a piece like that—and this would include any verse, too—do you approach that any differently than you would another role?

RR: Actually, Nicholas spoke in a mostly modern voice. And that was David Edgar. But all the great narrative passages which were shared by the company were straight from the book. His descriptions of people rolling down hills, scattering sheep. None of that was on stage. It was placed in the audience's mind through Dickens.

As for Shakespeare, if you're going to act him, you can't see his writing as poetry. Just get people to sit down and discuss for a minute what Shakespeare is. And once you get over that poetry thing, you can talk about what's really there. You can talk about the reality or the image of reality. Because Shakespeare is reality. Theatrical, yes. A sham, yes. I don't really break down in tears. I pretend to break down. That's craft. But the object is for people watching it to believe that it is reality. It's often achieved in Shakespeare these days by modernisms, tricks, craft things like pausing, speaking fast, speaking slow. Olivier, who was by no means naturalistic in Shakespeare, would throw away six lines in a second because he wanted you to listen to him say two words. He achieved a sort of naturalism through the theatrical.

RH: What is the most satisfying Shakespeare you've done?

RR: I don't have any favorites. I've always been reluctant to say this was good or that was bad. I don't know. I did enjoy playing Roderigo in *Othello.*

RH: Why?

RR: Oh, my canary died when I got to Cyprus.

RH: What?

RR: I was this librarian in Venice. And I brought a lot of stuff with me to Cyprus. And at the end of the first scene with Iago, in this very hot Cyprus, he notices that the canary is dead. Sort of portentous. John Barton directed, and did this wonderful thing: he had Iago try to black my face when we were going to assassinate Cassio. It was a great image.

RH: He's usually played as a sort of fop, Roderigo.

RR: Yeah, but this is a real guy. He's got to be real, or the audience won't care. Let's see . . . I was always playing parts like Aguecheek in *Twelfth Night*, and Gratiano in *Merchant*, and Claudio in *Much Ado*. They are difficult parts to make real. So I enjoyed that part of it. But for sheer enjoyment . . . ?

RH: Or satisfaction for *you*. I don't mean that you thought you were wonderful, but a satisfying experience.

RR: Well, Trevor Nunn's production of *The Comedy of Errors* was everything that I like about theatre.

RH: What part did you play?

RR: Antipholus of Syracuse. And Judi Dench was Adriana. It took place on a permanent set that we had that season, that was made to resemble one half of the Globe Theatre. But not in any patronizing way. It was just timber with a gallery. And it was decorated by John Napier to look like Ephesus today. There were T-shirt shops and two cafes and a little outside band. And we put a lot of music into it, songs. And at the end there was a chase. And on Friday and Saturday night in those towns in Greece, they show films on the square, and the film we showed was a cowboy film called *Call to Arms*. So there was this long, elaborate chase at the end which involved the whole company, and there was this cowboy chase going on in the film at the same time. And Michael Williams, who was my Dromio, would always call the chase *Call to Legs* because it was so hard to do. We finished up sliding down cables.

And we were doing *Macbeth* at the same time. Judi was playing Lady Macbeth. I was doing Malcolm. In *Winter's Tale*, I was the young shepherd. And all of these were done on the same set. It was thrilling. *Comedy of Errors* was probably performed originally as a divertissement. It has

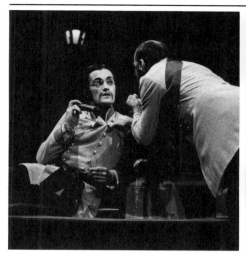

. . . with Emorys James as Iago in *Othello*, Royal Shakespeare Company, 1971 (*left*), with Michael Williams as Dromio in *Comedy of Errors*, Royal Shakespeare Company, 1977, (*right*). Photos © Joe Cocks Studio Collection, courtesy Shakespeare Centre Library.

wonderful, true lines, and you see the seeds of what would come later in *Pericles* and *The Tempest*:

> I to the world am like a drop of water,
> That in the ocean seeks another drop,
> Who, falling there to find his fellow forth,
> Unseen, inquisitive, confounds himself:
> So I, to find a mother and a brother,
> In quest of them, unhappy, lose myself.

Beautiful.

RH: I would have loved to see it.

RR: It was an experience.

RH: In the theatre, who are the directors you liked working with?

RR: Trevor. Peter Wood. Arthur Lane, who directed the first play I did professionally. He was one of the last of the English actor/managers. Arthur simply tore up the pages of Samuel French and left them all over the stage, and he moved about when he needed the words. Peter Wood is a thrilling director. Full of malice and scorn and a deep, deep love of the theatre and great acting. He's got a marvelous venom about him. You have to steel yourself because he attacks. But it's worth it because he's got a great wisdom which is different from anyone else I've worked with. He's too fond of actors to let on how fond he is.

RH: You worked a lot with Trevor Nunn.

RR: Trevor had the great fortune to do many tremendous things after the years when we worked together. But he guided my career. I was in the second production he did with the RSC and I was in the last one, and in the middle somewhere was *Nickleby*. And as he grew as a director, I had more and more opportunities within the company.

RH: What makes Trevor Nunn a great director?

RR: He described himself once like this, and it was with reference to *Nickleby*: "I'm not a director. I'm just a guide. Now anyone can say, let's go along this path here. But after thirty miles, I'm going to be the one who says, 'No, we have to go back to the starting point.'" He has two great qualities. He is the infinite master of compromise, and he has a remarkable ability to describe epic moments in small domestic situations. And he really knows how to tell a story with clarity and drama. I guess that's *three* great qualities. He will use the moving of a prop in such a way that it will make you know that Rome has fallen. He's very warm, very affectionate, and he's probably the silliest person I know.

RH: Well, I think you have to have a fund of silliness to get along in this business.

RR: That's for sure. People who put too great a value on their own importance are frightening to me.

RH: Have you ever had an experience with a director that you really didn't like?

RR: I was talking to Jane Carr the other day—she's doing *Small Family Business* now—and I asked her about a director she had worked with a couple of years ago, and she said, "Him? Don't worry. He won't get in your way." Of course, I'm much too discreet to mention any names, but sometimes your heart sinks when you realize a director hasn't got a clue. Then again, directors probably feel that way about their actors on occasion.

RH: What's the worst thing that ever happened to you on stage?

RR: I was at an interview the other day in Los Angeles, and this guy came up to me and said, in front of a lot of people who were sitting around, "Oh, I saw your Hamlet . . ." And I was quite pleased, and everyone looked up from their newspapers, and I thought, well, good, now they know I've played Hamlet. And then he completed the sentence. ". . . the night your codpiece fell off." That's the worst, I guess. Usually I have a great deal of fun on stage.

RH: Do you think there's really a place for critics in the theatre, and if so, what is it?

RR: Sure. Absolutely. The people who have spent some time actually thinking about what they think, thinking about context, and writing well—they're fine. But I think critics should contribute, rather than denigrate. There's probably a place where critics could really join in more than they already do. We should make them our allies rather than our adversaries.

It's not like critics are exclusive to the theatre and film. There are scientific critics, literary critics. Ellen Terry said—I think it was when George Bernard Shaw died—she said she was so glad he wouldn't say anything mean about her again . . . but she would miss what he said about other people.

RH: Before we have to close, I'd like to change the subject for a moment. What do you see as the chief difference between acting on the stage and acting for camera?

RR: I don't think there's too much difference. The technique is different, I suppose.

RH: What do you mean?

RR: In big theatres you have to wear black lines around your eyes so that the back of the house can see them. You have to project your voice so the balcony can hear your words. On film that's not necessary. Acting in a small, intimate one hundred and fifty-seat theatre is more like film.

Except you can feel the heat of the audience. You can feel them breathe. You can hear their heartbeats. You can also see when people aren't listening, when a critic is writing. And when they yawn at Playwrights Horizons, God forbid!, you sure know *that*!

You adapt your performance to different circumstances, but it's the technique that's different, not the actual acting. The emotional thrust has to have truth behind it, or it's not real. If we were performing what is going on in this room right now—you, me, the tape recorder, our feelings about the theatre—and we were doing it in a two thousand-seat theatre, we would still want the emotional content of the room to be based on truth. And if Martin Scorsese were beside us with a Steadicam, we'd still want the emotional dynamic of what we say to be based on truth. It's just a different way of portraying the same story.

There's now a whole generation and a half of actors who only know about acting for the camera. But you're talking to a stage actor who has done some films; and it's harder for someone who's done a lot of shouting in theatres, and a lot of lugging around of shields and furniture, to come in slightly under his energy, which is what it seems to me film acting is about.

RH: Do you have a film experience that you like a lot?

RR: Oh, yes. *Star 80*, the Bob Fosse film. I played the character based on Peter Bogdanovich, which we weren't supposed to say, but now I've said it.

RH: What did you like about it?

RR: Well, Gwen Verdon and I were talking yesterday, and she reminded me of what his technique with you was. He'd stick his head next to the lens—not just with me, but with everyone in the picture—and in the pauses when you weren't actually speaking, he'd say, "Don't act, Roger. Don't act." And it was like he was your conscience, watching out for you. It was great. He was very warm to me, very accepting, and I think he hired me for the role, sight unseen. It was after *Nicholas Nickleby* in New York. What I liked so much about him was his supreme sense of what he wanted and his joy in getting it. His frustration, too. He was a very committed man. It wasn't unlike the *Nickleby* experience. Working with great people is always great.

184

My experience with Bob Rafelson was similar. I was supposed to do a role in his *Mountains of the Moon*, and then the original actor scheduled for it was available again, and so, as a kind of consolation prize, he gave me a little scene at the end of the movie. And I'm very happy with that. It was this wonderful little scene, so poignant, so sad. And I spent two days with Bob Rafelson working on it. I ache to do that kind of detailed work again in film. Some days you go into the Studio, they give you a suit, and you hit your mark and then you go home. I've mostly played generic villains, because in America I speak with an accent. Villains with not a real link to the story other than that they're the bad guys. I suppose one should be more selective, but there's always that mortgage needing to be paid. I'm looking forward to doing movies where I can do what I do—like what we're approaching with Robbie Baitz's play—with a director who wants me at my best and a story we all care about telling. I've been lucky enough to have this a lot in the theatre, but I've yet to experience it fully in film.

Photo by Harry Langdon.

Like a Piece of Music

MADELINE KAHN

This interview took place on Friday, June 11, 1993, in the living room of Miss Kahn's upper east side Manhattan apartment. It was five days after she had won the Best Actress Tony Award for her performance as Gorgeous Teitelbaum in Wendy Wasserstein's *The Sisters Rosensweig*. I had watched her develop this character from the first time the play was read out loud (in February 1992) to its final incarnation at the Barrymore Theatre on Broadway. It is one of the chief reasons I wanted to interview her for this book. I had always felt Madeline Kahn was one of this country's finest comedians. Watching, close up, the precise, methodical way she found the rich inner life of this woman named Gorgeous is one of my most cherished memories as a stage manager. It was the purpose of this interview to capture how she did it.

Roy Harris: When you read a script and say to yourself, "I should do this role," what makes you feel that?

Madeline Kahn: Well, there are things that have nothing to do with the script. Those are not the things you want now, right?

RH: I'm interested in everything. You may decide to do something for a money reason. That's fine.

MK: Well, of course I have. And I hope people can tell which ones those are. But there are usually two considerations, though. First, the way the script strikes me and how I can relate to the part or *if* I can relate to it—if I feel it's really within the realm of possibility for me (not just something that people think I can do but which *I* don't think I can do). So there has to be some connection that I make to the part.

In addition to that, there is something that has nothing to do with the script (which actually does), and that is the people who are going to put it together. Especially in a play, and most especially in an off-Broadway play where you're going to be working hard and you're not going to be earning much money, you want it to be an experience that will be very fulfilling. And that depends, as you well know, as much on the people involved as it does on the script. So deciding to do a role is really a combination of those two things.

In our case with *The Sisters Rosensweig*, it was a chance to work with André Bishop at Lincoln Center, Dan Sullivan, and of course, Wendy Wasserstein. And I wanted to work on something new. So all those elements are very important.

RH: When you first read it—when they asked you to do the reading—what made you do it?

MK: You want total honesty, right?

RH: Absolutely. I want you to say what you really feel.

MK: I was afraid of doing this role.

RH: Why?

MK: I think it may have to do with the fact that I am a Jewish woman, and I'm very sensitive to doing stereotype sketches of Jewish women. And, right off the page, I thought that the role of Gorgeous had the danger of being that. When I first read it, I couldn't imagine a real individual saying those words unless she was campy. And I didn't want to come to Lincoln Center, be in a new play with all these talented people, and be the campy one. But I felt they're such smart people, they will have the answer to this. Anyway, just for the reading in February, I decided to do a surface version of a few women I've known in life who are very likable, very intelligent, but do have some of these stereotypical qualities. Now after the reading, I heard from many people. "You were so funny," they said. "You have to do this part." And I thought, 'I was? I do?' Later, Wendy and Dan asked me to come in and read the darker sections for them. I don't mind doing that because I wanted to see what

188

Madeline Kahn as Gorgeous Teitelbaum arriving in her faux Chanel at her sister's London home, Barrymore Theatre, 1993. Photo by Martha Swope.

it would feel like with Dan, because I knew I would want his help with that aspect. So, mostly I decided to play Gorgeous because everyone thought I should do it. I take my cues from the universe, too, not only from inside myself.

RH: Now, we went into rehearsal last August and you started working on who she was. Do you do a lot of homework?

MK: Well, first of all, from the minute I know I'm going to do a project, I'm working on it all the time. The good thing about doing something like *The Sisters Rosensweig* is that you do have some time. So you're free to let it roll around in your brain. Before we started rehearsal I sat down and read it very slowly; I just read it over and over, with great concentration. But from that point on, it's in my brain, and my computer is at work on it. And it's an ongoing process from the moment I know I'm going to be doing it until well after the reviews are out and I'm sure I know what it is. And it never stops. It becomes almost tormenting. And you think, 'Am I ever going to stop thinking about this?' And then you just do. There comes a point where you can forget about it until you get to the theatre.

RH: Before you go into rehearsal do you think about how this person looks?

MK: The external things you mean?

RH: Yes.

MK: Definitely.

RH: And does that affect how you work in rehearsal?

MK: Everything occurs to me. I don't sit down and think about just one thing, like the *look*. But since there were many specific things said in the script about the kind of clothes Gorgeous wears—the brand of clothes, her jewelry, and her accessories—I was worried that her look might detract from the possibility of my doing a sensitive performance. Now I saw very early that no one had strong notions about that, which meant it was open to my interpretation. So, yes I thought about it a lot. I did think it was important that those outward elements be there—the physical cues that tell you, "Oh, look, this is who she is." And, yet, that they not be so dominant that they distract you from her.

RH: I know what you're saying. One of the reasons I'm asking about this is that I think Gorgeous' first costume is a brilliant creation. It's one of the chief reasons, I think, that Jane Greenwood got a Tony nomination for the show. It gets all the things you need to know about her from an external point of view—she's not wearing the real thing, there's something a little too *much* about this person—but it doesn't overwhelm you so that you can't see the person underneath.

MK: That's exactly right. Jane was very sensitive to the way Gorgeous should look. That costume even has some classic references.

190

. . . modeling *the real thing* in *The Sisters Rosensweig*, Barrymore Theatre, 1993. Photo by Martha Swope.

RH: What do you mean?

MK: That little polka dot blouse. Now who would wear that? No one. But it's very *Harlequin-ish*, or perhaps very *Commedia-ish*. Well, at least I look somewhat *Commedia* in that blouse.

RH: From a spectator's point of view, Gorgeous' clothes get less showy as the play goes on. Were you aware of that as you and Jane looked at clothes?

MK: No, not as you put it. But Jane was very pleased because I always chose the more subtle choices she offered. As the scenes got more complicated, I felt you wanted to see more of *her*. For instance, the Chanel suit we chose is not typical of Chanel. The one we picked was the subtlest, most heavenly one. When I put most Chanel suits on, I look boxy and amusingly suburban. And that's not what you want there. The point of that scene is the ecstasy of that divine gift and her great pleasure when she puts it on. Now, I felt very fortunate to be in the company of people like Jane, Dan, and Wendy, who desired to show the inner part of this woman.

RH: To have approached her any other way would be to ruin her. It would be a terrible mockery because Gorgeous is a great character.

MK: Well, now she's taken her place alongside Anna Christie and Michael Redgrave's daughter.

RH: When I first read the play, I was most moved by Gorgeous.

MK: No kidding?

RH: Yes, because when she gets the thing she most wants, she gives it away. The generosity of it made me cry. My response probably has to do with my being a parent, and Gorgeous' giving up this $10,000 outfit so that one of her children can go to college in the fall.

MK: Now that's interesting, because when I read it, it showed me that she's not a stereotype. I happen to know a lot of Jewish women about whom you would come to conclusions based on their appearance. But, like Gorgeous, if their husbands suffered reversals, they'd be out there doing whatever was necessary. These women are resilient; they're ethical, strong, loyal, responsible, and they'd be there for you in a hard time or a good time. But, you know, Gorgeous gives the Chanel suit back partly for a practical reason: it solves a problem in her life. She feels, "Well, now that's solved."

RH: Now in working on Gorgeous, did you do any sort of research?

MK: Well, for the candlelighting ceremony, yes, I did. I didn't have any firsthand experience with the lighting of the Shabbes candles, and the character did. So I asked the mothers of friends of mine, and they

192

agreed to tape themselves saying the prayer and even explaining what each word meant. Also, two friends of my mother agreed to videotape the ceremonies in their homes, which was a very nice personal touch. Now being a New Yorker, I could easily have gone to any synagogue and seen this, but I wanted it to be through my mother in some way, so it would feel *firsthand*, authentic.

And then, of course, we had Rabbi Schnier come into one rehearsal, and he validated, for me, that I knew what I was doing. It was very important (because of who she is) that Gorgeous look like she knew what she was doing. Do you know what I mean?

RH: Oh, of course. When you do other roles do you often research?

MK: Yeah, particularly if it's something I don't know much about.

RH: Do you do whatever research you feel is required?

MK: I do it because it's useful, and sometimes I do it because it sparks your imagination and enriches the source of your creativity.

RH: When you're in rehearsal, what are you looking for from other actors? What is an ideal, or good, rehearsal situation for you?

MK: The best thing is some kind of heartfelt connection so that you can exchange feelings freely. You can then choose the ones that will be the real ones for the role. And so you hope that the other actors you're working with will be open to that.

RH: Was *The Sisters Rosensweig* a good rehearsal situation for you?

MK: Well, actually it wasn't ideal, but they rarely are. Dan has a mind set that, for me, wasn't always easy. I think he expected you to do what you had to do, and he would edit it. And that's fine . . . just not easy for me. I was uncomfortable wondering, will I get there? how will I get there? And I knew the other actors' way of working was different. Bob Klein is a different kind of actor. Jane Alexander is, too. She will definitely get there, but what you see in rehearsal is her technical expertise. That's how she works.

So I decided, at one point, that I had to bring it in myself and risk being self-conscious. I have to find out in rehearsal how it's going to work. So there was one day when I knew I'd be doing the scene with the broken shoe. I don't know if you remember it, but I seemed upset to everyone, and I was. And it was deliberate. I knew I had to do that scene as deeply as I could there, in order to find out how to do it. So I didn't have fun. And that's okay.

RH: When you work on a role—any role—how much do you consciously use things that have happened in your life to understand a character?

MK: I use anything that comes into my mind, anything that will lead me where I have to be. There is a place where I know, this is the place I have to be, this works now. It not only gets me logically from point A to point B, but it gets me from the beginning to the end. The pathway is right. It's really hard finding the pathway. But whatever puts me and keeps me on the path, I use.

RH: When you're finding the path, how conscious is that in your homework and in your rehearsal work?

MK: What do you mean by conscious?

RH: Are you saying, "Okay, now I'm going to work on this scene so I can find what she's after and how she gets it?"

MK: Yes, I attack it like a piece of music.

RH: Great. What do you mean by that?

MK: With a piece of classical music, you already know it works. But in order to be the one to perform it, you still have to take the music totally apart. It's not just learning the notes (that's obvious, it's like learning lines). You have to find what inside you is going to make your voice go from that note to that note. And what is it inside of you that's going to allow you to start on those notes and then soar up to those other notes. Where do you have to be *inside* to take you through those notes? Of course you have to sing them technically, but you have to know who the person is who is singing these lyrics.

And so, with a scene you ask: where has this person just been? what are the realities of her life at that moment? what is on her mind? It's like you and me sitting here now. A person comes to any situation, and there are things present in your life that are going on in the back of

194

your mind. There's your physical situation that day. All of those things that I'm not telling you about—what happened to me last night, a phone call I may have had—well, they color everything I say.

Now, none of that is on the page, though there are a lot of clues. So I have to imagine myself into the situation of this woman named Gorgeous. She has four children. I figure two of them are out of the house by now; the other two are still at home. Her husband is really not able to be much of a father at this time. I'm constructing the outer life of this woman that will tell me what her emotional life is.

"I was walking around in this neighborhood. I came out of a store and something was leaking, and a little of it got on me. And for some reason, it made me cry. And I thought, 'Ah, stay with this feeling.' And you stay with it, see where it takes you, and you get into the right emotional groove, and then say the lines."

For instance, there's her entrance with the broken shoe. She's supposed to be drenched. How do you get to that feeling? Well, there was a day when I was walking around in this neighborhood. I came out of a store and something was leaking, and a little of it got on me. And for some reason, it made me cry. And I thought, 'Ah, stay with this feeling.' And you stay with it, see where it takes you, and you get into the right emotional groove, and then say the lines.

RH: This is just fascinating. When you said it's like music—to me your performance as Gorgeous is like music. There's a rhythm that's always there underneath it. It'll vary because of something different you get from the audience or another cast member. But that basic rhythm I always see there, and to me it's like music. It's really a character rhythm.

MK: You could put it that way. Could be. It's also the writing itself.

RH: Another question: you mentioned earlier that at a certain point you got to the feeling that you knew what you were doing. Now you've done Gorgeous almost three hundred times. Is it harder now or easier?

MK: It's different. In the beginning when you aren't sure of it yet— either you're still finding it, or you think it will work but maybe it won't, or the director is still checking it out so you're still being judged—at that point there's so much adrenaline before you go on, the adrenaline does carry you, even if there's discomfort.

Your life on stage is energized because you are in a condition of striving and searching and proving. And that energy propels you around the stage and creates this tension which is felt as excitement by the audience. And your task then is to find the things which work best and which withstand that energy going through you all the time.

And then that subsides because you've found it. You landed, you're there, and everything's okay. And then you no longer have that disturbing energy propelling you. Your task, however, is to maintain it anyway. And you hope you're with a group of people who know that they have to find another way of creating that energy. Comedy absolutely requires the motor, the energy. It really does not work without it. It's not like a drama. The drama itself supports it.

Your task as a stage actor is to find something in that moment that will propel you through and give you the same results. And sometimes it's sheerly technical. Thank God there's something called technique that carries you through. It's a different energy.

RH: Now, I've noticed that you are very methodical. You come down at exactly the same time every night, you go to the change booth, you sit in your chair, and you stand up, cross to the door, and pick up the shopping bags at the same time. Is all of that part of what makes it work for you each night?

MK: Well, it seems to be. Doesn't everyone do that?

RH: No. Everyone is different.

MK: I'm such a creature of habit.

RH: Why shouldn't you be if it works for you? There are some people who come over and chat before they enter.

196

MK: I could never do that.

RH: No, you wouldn't. There are others who race right to their entrance. Now as a stage manager I can't say that thrills me, but it's their way, and as long as they get there, I'm not going to judge.

MK: You know what? I think I work partly the way a dancer works.

RH: What do you mean?

MK: Well, dancers are musicians too. I've established certain nerve pathways in the playing of the role, and if I get off to the right start, it'll just go. It's really like a train going on a track, and I just have to feed in these little, current things to keep it sparking along. But, you know, part of what's hard about my role is that there are these twenty-minute intervals in between.

RH: Well, that is hard.

MK: You come on in high gear, or you come on and you get into high gear very quickly, you leave in high gear, and then you have twenty minutes (or sometimes thirty, with the intermission), and you come back on again. Now I have established what the notes are, what the levels are, and I have to be able to click into it when I return to the stage, or I won't get to where I have to. It's so much easier to do a role where the scene builds logically because it's a conversation. I say this, you say that, and the lines bring you to where you need to go. Gorgeous has very little of that. Something triggers her and she has to be *there*. In that way it's a virtuoso role, and it requires virtuosity (which is what makes it musical, like a concerto). It has arias.

RH: Well, a little like Rhadames. He comes in singing at the top of his register for "Celeste Aida."

MK: Marilyn Horne said there are these Bel Canto operas that Rossini wrote for a contralto coloratura—perhaps he wrote them for one woman. Well, they are now sitting on a shelf somewhere because very few people can do them. They require virtuosity.

RH: I'm switching the subject briefly. Do you think there's a true place for critics in the theatre, and if so, what is it?

MK: Well, the information has to get out to the public. Everyone sees things differently and has different tastes. But the thing I don't like about some critics is they have a small palette. For instance, if we didn't know what foods were edible and what ones would poison us, and we depended on certain critics to tell us, we would all be eating nothing but the white meat of turkey. Nothing green, for instance: "Oh, it's green. Ugh!" And all the many foods which are fine would be listed as inedible.

RH: Now, if you were going to do Gorgeous in the movie, is there anything that you would do differently?

MK: Well, I think I'd have to rethink it. First, I'd have to let it clear out of my system because I've established this routine with her. But it can be done. Just lately I've seen Mercedes Ruehl achieve it. Her performance in *Lost in Yonkers* is as good or better than it was on the stage. Irene Worth, too, even more so. The camera can come in and pick up these little things that happen on your face, and you'd never see it in the theatre. There's a different physical reality on stage.

RH: What do you mean by that?

MK: Well, on stage your method of transmitting the material is more active. You are the transmitter. You have to send out the message, to project it. For instance, on stage if you know they can't see your face or it's covered for some reason, you have to do something with your body that will transmit it. There's this one line I have and I have to accompany it with a gesture like this, to let them know that the sentence isn't finished yet.

RH: It's when you say, "I haven't been this happy since the day I found out that I made cheerleader and I knew that Sara didn't."

MK: Right, and when I started getting the laugh after "cheerleader," I found myself making that gesture to let them know I'm going to keep on talking so they wouldn't miss the rest of the line. Since you are the mechanical means by which the message is sent out—rather than a camera picking it up—you use your whole physical self in addition to the truth of the character.

RH: Since you mentioned the word *classic* earlier, is there any classic role you'd like to play?

MK: I think I would like to do something classical but I'm not at all sure what it would be. You know, though, it's very important to me to do new works and help to turn them into classics. I always try to find the classic reference in anything I do. For instance, in *Paper Moon* it was definitely Tennessee Williams. And once I realized that, I worked on the role with the depth of Williams in mind. In *Blazing Saddles*, the reference was Bertolt Brecht-Kurt Weill and Ernst Lubitsch movies (added into Mel Brooks). I try, wherever I can, to find the classic vein to tap into.

RH: Well, I think you've definitely helped turn some new plays into classics. I'm sure that *The Sisters Rosensweig* will be seen one day as a classic. There are many reasons for that, and your performance as Gorgeous has helped insure that.

MK: Well, thank you.

RH: As far as I can tell, your winning the Tony is about your future work. People will finally see—and too bad it took an award to do it—what a fine dramatic actress you are. The Tony will give you a new kind of clout.

MK: And who knows what that will mean?

In That One Specific Moment

VICTOR GARBER

Victor Garber talks about acting technique and his own way of working with the same energy and style that he brings to every role I've ever seen him play. The subject becomes vigorously immediate, so much so that anyone reading it would understand something of what acting is about. Like Charles Durning whose interview began this book, Victor Garber "never studied a specific technique." This fact does not seem to stand in his way. A vivid sense of life itself and the inevitable theatricality of life permeates the interview. It took place on Tuesday, November 24, 1992, in the stage manager's office of the Mitzi Newhouse Theater at Lincoln Center, a few days before Victor Garber flew to Toronto a play an unscrupulous agent in the film *Life with Mikey*.

Roy Harris: When you read a script and say to yourself, 'I have to do this role,' what makes you feel that?

Victor Garber: It's usually an emotional response. And it's mostly impressionistic, not specific. Often I think, 'Oh, I couldn't do this. I'd never be able to do it.' The last time I felt this was when I read *Two Shakespearean Actors* by Richard Nelson. I wanted to do it because it excited me just as an event, and I was also moved by it. I actually thought, though, 'I don't know how you do this play,' and I felt that way up until the last week I played it. You know, there are really all sorts of different considerations, like: eight times a week, who else is working on it; who is actually on stage with me; who will I be living with for six to eight months? As a young actor I never even thought about that.

RH: Now, last season you did *Two Shakespearean Actors* and a couple of seasons before that you did *Lend Me a Tenor*. Very different. One's a period statement about theatre, actors, and acting, and the other's a farce. What made you do that?

VG: I did *Lend Me a Tenor* because it was directed by Jerry Zaks. When I know that I am in safe hands, when I know that I'm going to be protected as an actor, it's much easier to jump in even if there are some doubts. I also knew that this material was completely within Jerry's grasp.

RH: Now, you've worked with Jerry Zaks three times: *Lend Me a Tenor*, *Wenceslas Square*, and *Assassins*. What is he like to work with?

VG: I find Jerry an enormously exciting director. I would work with him anytime. You know, the important thing is what the dynamic is. Whatever people think about acting, it's a collaboration. And if it isn't, it's not very interesting to me. The dynamic that I have felt with Jerry is that I am challenged, excited, and he makes me laugh. And that is a really important element for me. I ask, will this be fun?

RH: Absolutely. It's one of my first criteria. And it's why I love working with Dan Sullivan and Wendy Wasserstein. I can't tell you what a good time it is.

VG: I'm sure. I'm looking for a general sense of: am I in good hands with the writer, the director, the producer, the costumer? Those elements are so important to me. When I know that Tony Walton, Paul Gallo, Jane Greenwood, or William Ivey Long are involved, that definitely moves me much closer to doing something than the actual character itself.

RH: When you get the role—Edwin Forrest in *Two Shakespearean Actors* or Max in *Lend Me a Tenor*—and you've got, say, three weeks before rehearsals start, do you do any work beforehand?

VG: You know, I have no one way of doing it. It's different with every role. With Edwin Forrest I did a lot of work on it.

RH: What kind of work?

Victor Garber with Jennifer Van Dyck in Richard Nelson's *Two Shakespearean Actors*, Cort Theatre, Lincoln Center Theater production, 1992. Photo by Brigitte Lacombe.

VG: I read a lot of biographical material. The acting teacher, Michael Howard, loaned me books and photographs. He was very interested in that whole period and knew a lot about it. And I worked with a Shakespeare teacher at Michael's studio, Eloïse Watt. She was terrific. I was so petrified of those speeches from *Metamora* (which was one of the hardest things I've ever done), and then from both *Macbeth* and *King Lear*. I mean, I had never played any of the great Shakespearean roles, and I was going to be working with Brian Bedford (as Macready) who'd done them all. Of course, I was intimidated.

But I realized that even though I had to do all these scenes from Shakespeare within the play itself, you approach it the same way you approach any role: who is this guy? what does he want? where is he going? and what does he need to get there? And it doesn't matter if you're speaking verse or not. I had moments where I'd feel, 'That's closer,' or 'That felt right,' and, you know, that was the great thing about doing that play: it never stopped challenging me. And, of course, what Shakespeare gives you is: the more you peel away the more you have, and the more you reveal, the more you need to peel away. So, Edwin Forrest was probably the most challenging and one of the most exciting roles in my career.

RH: With a role like Max in *Lend Me a Tenor*, which is basically farce, did you do anything before rehearsals to prepare for it?

VG: You get in the best physical shape you can. You know, Max was another kind of challenge. I did it for almost a year. There's nothing easy in the theatre, and when I'm teaching I realize that most young people have no idea where you have to *go* in order to do it.

RH: One of the things I'd love for people to see from the interviews in this book is just how much hard work there is in acting. People just don't know.

VG: No, you're right. And that's because a wonderful production looks easy. Look at your show, *The Sisters Rosensweig*. It just flows along, and I know how much went into it. I knew the play before; I see all the changes. I know those actors and how hard they work to make it look that way. But you know, the only people who have to know how hard it is are people getting into the business who think it's all fun and games.

RH: You said that you did Max for a year. Do you have anything specific that you do to maintain it night after night?

VG: I think I've learned how to do it. It's a state of mind. I think it takes practice and a conscious awareness of what you're doing to remain fresh. I think a lot of physical exercise is important. I don't mean jogging necessarily. I mean any physical movement that you use to maintain contact with your body. It's crucial. Vocal exercises are also crucial. And attitude. You know, I'll never forget what Marian Seldes said one day when she came in for a Wednesday matinee of *Deathtrap*. I was dragging myself around, and Marian sort of sashayed into the theatre, in mauve, smelling wonderful as she always did, and she said to me, "Oh, my darling, we get to do it twice today." And she did the role for five years.

I thought to myself that day, 'what does it take to shift my attitude to hers?'

RH: Let's back up a little. When you get into rehearsal, and it's day three, do you do any homework at night before?

". . . what Shakespeare gives you is: the more you peel away, the more you have, and the more you reveal, the more you need to peel away."

VG: It's very basic: I learn my lines because until I know them I can't do much of anything. I'm also a stickler for learning word perfect. Now that gets me closer and closer to the person I'm playing. Also, I look at the scene I'm about to rehearse and I start to dissect it and ask: what's really going on here? where does this come from? why do you think he's doing this? I have never studied a specific technique, and I'm envious of people who know how to break down a script into beats. Actually, I think I do it. I just do it my own way.

RH: Are you more an instinctive actor or one more given to plan?

VG: Everybody's both. But if I had to choose, I'd say instinctive. Although, you know, I'm really meticulous. I don't know exactly where that comes from, but I'm uncomfortable with any messy edges. And that isn't always good. But I think, given the kind of actor I am and the kind of roles I've played, it's served me well. I don't like messy acting. I don't like acting that is without some kind of technical discipline. There are people who think that acting is just about emoting. If you can cry or if you can show a lot of big emotion, then you can act. That's the kind of acting I loathe. I've actually probably patterned myself more on an English style of acting. I don't want to box myself in here, though.

RH: And I don't want you to box yourself in. This is investigative. The way an actor sees himself is fascinating, even if it's different from what I think I see. Your feeling about yourself is very important.

VG: I do struggle every day of my life to be authentic, and that's what I've taken over to the theatre.

RH: When you're in rehearsal, what are you looking for from other actors? What do you want in a rehearsal situation?

VG: Support, spontaneity, truth. No games, in that way that we can sometimes do, you know. And I have a really good nose for people who do that and people who don't, and it's partly what determines whether I'll take a role or not.

RH: What is a good rehearsal situation you've been in?

VG: I've been in many good ones, but I'd say *Two Shakespearean Actors.* I loved the play, the director, the actors, and the designers. And it was a completely collaborative event. I'm not saying there weren't days when I wanted out, and there were many times when I felt I was unequal to the task. I feel positive about it now because I really did get a handle on this guy before it closed, and I don't often say that. Not long before it closed, believe me. About a week. I had had a cold off and on through the run, and I wasn't in a very good emotional state, but I finally felt I understood something of him. That was a very rewarding feeling.

I also think I lost, at least for a while, that awful sense of constantly needing other people's approval. That is really the hardest thing for me. Of course you want people to like it, you want friends to come back and say it was wonderful. But it got to a point with *Two Shakespearean Actors* as it did with *Assassins* (and believe me, people would come back after that one and just stare at you) that a given in this situation is that people aren't always going to know what to make of it, and it doesn't really matter. The most important thing is *my perception of what I'm doing,* and that has to be my focus.

RH: You've mentioned two different directors now: Jerry Zaks and Jack O'Brien. Are they alike as directors or different?

VG: The thing they have in common—and they are quite different— is that they are both in control. And that's what I want from a director. Someone whom I'm not going to be able to take advantage of, and who will make sure it's not going to fall apart. It's a rare thing in a director.

206

Basically what they do is create an ensemble. The best theatre is when everybody is good.

RH: And we don't see that all that often.

VG: No, we don't. Jerry and Jack both create that ensemble feeling. Also, they both have a sense of fun.

I would say that Jerry, right off the bat, hears the music in his head and knows exactly what he wants. And he's right most of the time. Because I trust Jerry so implicitly and we've worked together, I am really putty in his hands. And that's why we work so well together. I'm comfortable with him. He's not telling me how to play the part. He's like a conductor, and it's very evident in his productions. And I love that.

With Jack, it evolves differently in rehearsal. He was relentlessly positive, and just as you felt you were stepping on ice floes that were going in different directions—and I really felt that way a great deal of the time I was playing Forrest—Jack never wavered or lost his focus. So they were two very good experiences.

RH: Is there any difference in your approach when you're playing a real person like Forrest as opposed to a fictional person like Max? I'm asking this because of something Julie Harris said when I talked with her.

VG: That's a hard one to answer because I played (in film) Liberace, Hemingway, and then Jesus.

RH: Quite a combination, those three!

VG: Yeah, quite. Once I got over the idea that I had to live up to someone else's notion of these people, there really is no difference in approaching them. You have to go where the author takes you. It's really one man or one woman's idea of who this person is. So all the biographical material in the world may be very useful or it could make you completely insane. Inevitably, I stop in the middle of all that and just go back to the script and ask: what's going on in this scene? what do I want? Hopefully, the embroidery from all the reading will filter through in some way. But it should never be evident.

RH: You've mentioned specific designers several times. How affected are you by the costumes you're going to wear?

VG: Oh, completely. I think it's a major thing, and the set, too. This is where you are going to be living every day. I'm not a big clothes person in my life. Clothes are sometimes just a nuisance to me. I never know what to wear half the time. So when I go into a play, I'm very amenable to what a designer wants me to wear.

RH: Have you ever had a costume that helped you enormously with the character when you first put it on?

VG: Well, I haven't actually had just that experience but I certainly have at some moment in a production thought, 'Ah, this works so well now.' For instance, the coat that William Ivey Long designed for John Wilkes Booth in *Assassins* was a great coat. (I should mention Vincent Costumes, too, because though William designed it, Vincent made it, and it fit me so beautifully.) And then Jane Greenwood designed the Liberace costumes. And, needless to say, put on those sequins and something sure happens inside you.

RH: Well, exactly what did those costumes for Liberace do?

VG: They fused the person with my idea of who he was. You ask, 'Who would wear these clothes?' You put them on, and it changes you. Who other than Liberace would wear those particular sequins, that particular color? It's really like doing a period play. The director says, get some shoes, and to the women, get corsets on. And by God, it changes you. It changes your relation to other people.

RH: You've had a major career in musical theatre. When you approach a role like Anthony Hope in *Sweeney Todd*, is it any different from how you approach, say, Edwin Forrest?

VG: I'd say yes.

RH: How?

VG: Musical theatre generally has it's own—really a different form of—reality. I think both have to be approached in a similar way, and then musical theatre takes on another dimension. In order to fill the requirements of musical theatre, you have to go to a place that is not

208

. . . with Jonathan Hadary (left) and Terrence Mann (right) in Stephen Sondheim's *Assassins*, Playwrights Horizons, 1990–91 season. Photo Martha Swope.

always comfortable, at least not for me. Musically, and this is certainly true of Sondheim, when you are given notes and words to sing, you have to follow those exactly. When it's just dialogue, you are bringing a lot of your own elements to it. So somehow you have to fuse those things—the specific notes—with what you bring. This must sound strange.

RH: No, it makes sense to me.

VG: My feeling is that everything in theatre has to be approached from this basis: do you believe what I'm doing? Unless you believe it, it's not working. That goes for a song or for a musical comedy performance. To me the greatest performances in musical theatre are always because they are truthful. Take Bernadette Peters and Mandy Patinkin in *Sunday in the Park with George* or Patti Lupone in *Evita*. I think all three of them are great artists in musical theatre. Jonathan Hadary in *Gypsy*—wonderful performance. So you do start at the same place, but in musical theatre the parameters are wider.

RH: I read your piece about Sondheim in the Broadway Cares/Equity Fights Aids book *Broadway, Day and Night*, and that's what makes me ask this. You've sung, arguably, two of the most beautiful songs that Stephen Sondheim ever wrote: "Johanna" from *Sweeney Todd* and "The Ballad of Booth" from *Assassins*. What does it feel like to have originated those two songs?

VG: Well, that's it. Stephen Sondheim is one of the reasons I am in this profession. I am touched by his work in a way that I rarely am. So to have an opportunity to work with him three times now, it's three experiences I cherish. The last was the revival of *Merrily We Roll Along* at Arena Stage last year. He gives you everything you need.

You know, one of the great experiences of my life was singing "The Ballad of Booth" at Carnegie Hall in the Tribute to Sondheim that was a benefit for Carnegie Hall.

RH: What was that like?

VG: There I was on stage with Patrick Cassidy, with an orchestra of fifty people behind us, with everybody in the business out there and knowing it was going to be televised this March. I had to ask myself, 'What am I singing about?' It's so easy to be overwhelmed by the circumstances that I had to remember: I just have to go out there and *mean what I say*.

RH: Also it must be hard to do out of context.

VG: But that is where Stephen Sondheim gives you the gift. If you surrender to his music, he's really done it for you. All I had to do was connect in a full way to what he had written, and I felt I achieved what I set out to do that evening.

RH: You've implied several times that you are not satisfied with your work. Do you think the dissatisfaction is part of what makes you good?

VG: I don't know. Maybe.

RH: Or put it differently: does your dissatisfaction imply that you're constantly working for something more?

VG: Well, that is true. And I think that's what keeps anybody alive. Period. Well, that's my life. It happens to carry over into my work. Sometimes I get discouraged and bogged down and think it's just bull. So the fact that I'm still trying is important; I'm still struggling to get better, yes.

"Stephen Sondheim is one of the reasons I am in this profession. . . . You know, one of the great experiences of my life was singing 'The Ballad of Booth' at Carnegie Hall in the Tribute to Sondheim . . ."

RH: What do you see as the chief difference between acting on stage and acting for a camera?

VG: You know, chiefly it's the circumstances.

RH: What do you mean?

VG: The physical circumstances. As opposed to being on stage in a theatre, you have a camera in your face. That governs what you will do, and how you will do it and say it. If you are on stage doing a performance, that night will be different from any other night. You play what you get from the other actors at that moment. Tomorrow they may look at you in a different way or respond to you differently.

So if you are on a sound stage on what is supposed to be a realistic set, it's going to require a different focus and a different response to the actual circumstances. If we're here talking, you can hear me without my raising my voice. But if we were doing this on a stage, I'd have to make an adjustment. Something I use all the time in teaching is what Jerry Zaks said once: "Make sure you need to be heard." That's a great simple note. So, the circumstances to a large degree dictate the different response. But I think that ultimately you go to the same place. I don't think that changes no matter what the circumstances are.

RH: When you do something for a movie or TV and you shoot out of sequence, how do you deal with that?

VG: It's a leap of faith in a lot of ways, I imagine. I think sometimes we underestimate our antennae. If you are playing fully the requirement of the scene, if you are in that moment, that's all you can do. You can't play anything of his past or what you know of his future. So actually it's not all that difficult. Of course it helps to know where you've been and where you're going. But ultimately that has to be forgotten. You must be in that one specific moment. I say to my students all the time, "You've never said what you are about to say and you've never heard the response to it."

So you have to be in that moment. And then you let go and let whatever those magical things are, happen. But what we're talking about now is one of the most crucial things about acting. Sometimes even with very accomplished actors, they will respond as they always have no matter what new things you might do. We are so in love with some things we do—and I'm guilty of this too—that we feel, "Oh, that was such a good line reading, that was so deep and wonderful, I'll do it that way again." And then you're really dead.

RH: Now I watched the miniseries that you did where you played Hemingway, and it's very Italian, which translates long and sluggish.

VG: Well, it's the Italian idea of Hemingway.

RH: I was struck, though, by the quality of the makeup in that film. You play him from age eighteen to age sixty. Can you tell me how that makeup helped you?

VG: Well, first, the whole thing was a bizarre experience. I was playing Ernest Hemingway and I was in Yugoslavia for most of the six months of filming. Fortunately, the director was good, and Walter Cossu, who did the makeup, was brilliant. Walter built every mustache, every beard from scratch. The longest makeup was about five hours when I was oldest and wore the bald cap and the wig over the bald cap. After five hours in a chair, you feel old anyway.

RH: When you looked at yourself in the mirror with the old age makeup, what did it make you feel?

VG: I thought first of my father, I felt sad, and I felt some of the things that people must feel when they're getting older. For instance, you don't feel inside the way you look.

. . . as Ernest Hemingway, age 18 (*left*), as Hemingway, age 40 (*center*), as Hemingway, age 60 (*right*) in the Italian television miniseries *Life of Ernest Hemingway*, 1988. Photos courtesy Victor Garber.

RH: What, physically, does the makeup do to you?

VG: Well, it pulls your skin down, the prosthetics do. It's painful, actually; it hurts while you wear it, and I think that helps with the aging, too. The combination of the actual weight of the makeup and the weight of this body suit that I wore when he was the oldest, both of those helped. The clothes, too, had a droop to them. But it was really a more internal thing. Getting out of that chair and looking at myself as this old man, I could see Hemingway.

RH: The thing that struck me about it was that, with each stage of the makeup, I could always see the young Victor/Ernest, no matter how old you got. I very rarely feel that about makeup. I could still see the eighteen-year-old inside the aging person.

VG: What makes Walter Cossu great is that beneath the layers of latex, he sees the humanity. He works relentlessly to make it real.

RH: What made you want to do the Liberace movie?

VG: I remember I was in Washington at the time doing *Wenceslas Square* and my agent called and said, "Well, I've got good news and bad news." I had never played a leading role in a TV movie, and it was a director I had done *Godspell* with. Also, a lot of well-known actors had turned it down, and so I thought, 'This is an impossible thing to do, so

213

I'll try it.' And it was exciting to me to have that kind of challenge and, also, to be frank, to make some money which I hadn't made in a while.

RH: Did you enjoy working on it?

VG: Yes and no. You really don't have time to enjoy it. Literally, I had two weeks to prepare for it.

RH: What sort of preparation did you do?

VG: I watched a lot of tapes, and the things that were most helpful were his old television shows. Again, as with Hemingway, I was playing him from a very young age. And I had to find something in him that I could find in myself. And it was a love of performing. And that's what I based the whole thing on.

RH: You mentioned to me once that you didn't care for the age makeup in that film. What sort of makeup did they use?

VG: Well, what I didn't like was they didn't have time. You can't afford four-and-a-half hours on a TV movie. The guys who did it were very good; it was just so rushed. It was a latex foundation, and then there were these teeth about which I was very resistant. My instinct is to trust people, and part of that comes from the fact that it takes too much energy not to trust. So there are things in the Liberace movie about which I thought, 'Oh, that's not really right.' But, there wasn't time. My goal for that movie was to bring dignity and humanity. Those were my two ideals.

RH: Well, you did. He looked and felt like a real person.

VG: Well, thanks.

RH: What's your favorite role you've ever played?

VG: You know, I don't have a favorite role. When I did Vernon in *They're Playing Our Song*, the Neil Simon/Marvin Hamlisch musical, it was a year-and-a-half of my life. It was a national tour, my first real starring role, and my first adult role. I had already done Clifford Anderson in *Death Trap* and Anthony Hope in *Sweeney Todd*, and those were good roles. But Vernon Gersh was a favorite because it was a big transition for me. Edwin Forrest marked another transition. But I think both have more to do with where I was at the time than with the role itself. Playing Vernon afforded me the opportunity to play an adult, neurotic, funny man. So it was the first time I felt, 'Oh, I can be funny. I didn't know I could be funny.' It was a huge transition for me.

RH: You've mentioned several times today your students. Do you like teaching?

VG: I do. I've stopped for a while. I taught at HB Studios and I did a summer project for a couple of weeks this summer. Often I don't really feel equipped to do it, but when I do it I find I am equipped. Acting can't be taught, but I think experiences can be shared. And you can advise to a certain degree. But as Sandy Meisner says, "The bottom line is talent." I think what I like most about teaching is that it forces me to get in touch with what I'm about. I realize I'm much more passionate about it than I thought I was. And when you see someone actually making a connection that they've never made before—it's like the Helen Keller "wa wa" moment—well, that is extremely rewarding. It must be what people having children feel all the time.

RH: This is an awful question to end with, but I'm going to ask anyway. Do you think that all the roles you've done are in you every time you do a new one?

VG: Oh, definitely.

RH: I do. When I look at you, I see Hemingway, I see John Wilkes Booth, I see Edwin Forrest, I see Max, I see Liberace, I see Anthony Hope, even old Jesus. All of these are in you and it cannot help but make for a certain sustained, largely unconscious, emotional depth, I'd think. There is a background of mind-work that you've done. Well, it's pretty amazing.

VG: I think, hopefully, that's what it's all about—at least partially. The greatest compliment I can receive as an actor is when people say to me, "You just get better." What else is there? But that's what I'm trying to do with my life: just get better. It's why I feel it's impossible to separate what you do from who you are.

Bios

The following biographical sketches, arranged in alphabetical order, are not intended to be complete, but rather to give an overview of each actor's career and, where necessary, to enhance the understanding of the interview itself. For instance, where a director or designer is referred to by first name in an interview, the full name is given under the biographical information for that play.

Stockard Channing

BROADWAY: *Four Baboons Adoring the Sun* by John Guare (Tony nomination, Best Actress), *Six Degrees of Separation* by John Guare, directed by Jerry Zaks, costumes designed by William Ivey Long (Tony nomination, Best Actress; Obie Award, Best Actress; Drama League Distinguished Performance Award, Drama Desk nomination), *They're Playing Our Song*, *The Rink*, *The Golden Age*, *The House of Blue Leaves* by John Guare, directed by Jerry Zaks, costumes designed by Ann Roth (Tony and Drama Desk nominations), *Love Letters* by A.R. Gurney, *Joe Egg* (Tony Award, Best Actress; Drama Desk and Outer Critics Circle nominations).

OFF-BROADWAY: *Woman in Mind* by Alan Ayckbourn (Drama Desk Award, Best Actress), *Lady and the Clarinet*.

FILM: Mike Nichols' *The Fortune* with Warren Beatty and Jack Nicholson, *Grease* (People's Choice Award), Stanley Jaffe's *Without a Trace*, Mike Nichols' *Heartburn*, *The Cheap Detective*, *Staying Together*, *Sweet Revenge*, *Meet the Applegates*, *Married to It*, *Six Degrees of Separation* (Academy Award nomination, Best Actress).

TELEVISION: *The Stockard Channing Show*, *Silent Victory*, Hallmark Hall of Fame's *The Room Upstairs*, CBS mini-series *Echoes in the Darkness* (Emmy nomination), *Tidy Endings* directed by Gavin Millar (ACE Award, Best Actress in a Dramatic or Theatrical Special) and HBO's *Perfect Witness* (Emmy nomination).

Charles Durning

BROADWAY: *Cat on a Hot Tin Roof*, directed by Howard Davies (Tony Award, Best Supporting Actor), *That Championship Season*, *The Au Pair Man* with Julie Harris, *In the Boom Boom Room* with Madeline Kahn, *Indians*, *The Happy Time*, *Drat the Cat*.

OFF-BROADWAY: *The Child Buyer, The World of Gunter Grass, The Happiness Cage, Two by Saroyan,* and thirty-five plays at Joseph Papp's Public Theatre over a twelve-year period.

REGIONAL: *Sweet Bird of Youth* with Joanne Woodward and Terry Kinney, *The Entertainer, Two for the Seesaw, The Three Sisters,* and *On Golden Pond* with Julie Harris.

FILM: *The Best Little Whorehouse in Texas* (Academy Award nomination, Best Supporting Actor), *To Be or Not to Be* with Anne Bancroft, directed by Mel Brooks (Academy Award nomination, Best Supporting Actor), *Tootsie, True Confessions* with Robert DeNiro and Robert Duvall, *The Muppet Movie, The Greek Tycoon, Mass Appeal, When a Stranger Calls,* and more than fifteen more.

TELEVISION: *Tales from Hollywood* directed by Howard Davies, *The Man Who Broke a Thousand Chains, Crisis at Central High* with Joanne Woodward, *Studs Lonigan,* and Emmy nominations for *Queen of the Stardust Ballroom, Attica, Captains and Kings,* and *Death of a Salesman.*

Victor Garber

BROADWAY: *Damn Yankees, Two Shakespearean Actors, Lend Me a Tenor* (Tony nomination), *The Devil's Disciple, You Never Can Tell, Deathtrap* (Tony nomination), *Little Me* (Tony nomination), *Noises Off, Sweeney Todd, Tartuffe, They're Playing Our Song.*

OFF-BROADWAY: *Assassins, Love Letters, Wenceslas Square* (Obie Award), *Ghosts* (Theatre World Award).

REGIONAL: *Merrily We Roll Aong* (Helen Hayes nomination), *Cyrano de Bergerac, As You Like It, The Winter's Tale, The Importance of Being Earnest, The Miser.*

FILM: *Kleptomania, Sleepless in Seattle, Life with Mikey, Singles, Light Sleeper, Godspell.*

TELEVISION: *The Grand Larceny, The First Circle, Liberace: Beyond the Music, The White Whale: Life of Ernest Hemingway* (Italian television film), *I Had Three Wives, Valley Forge, Roanoke, The Days and Nights of Molly Dodd.*

Julie Harris

BROADWAY: *The Member of the Wedding, I Am a Camera* (Tony Award), *The Lark* (Tony Award), *The Country Wife, A Shot in the Dark, The Au Pair Man* (Tony nomination), *Marathon '33* (Tony nomination), *Skyscraper* (Tony nomination), *Forty Carats* (Tony Award), *The Last of Mrs. Lincoln* (Tony Award), *The Belle of Amherst* (Tony Award), *Lucifer's Child* (Tony nomination).

OFF-BROADWAY: Tim Mason's *The Fiery Furnace* at Circle Rep.

NATIONAL TOURS: *The Warm Peninsula, And Miss Reardon Drinks a Little, Driving Miss Daisy, Lettice and Lovage.*

REGIONAL: *Bronte, Is He Still Dead? Under the Ilex, Tusitala, The Countess.*

FILM: *The Member of the Wedding* (Academy Award nomination), *I Am a Camera*, *East of Eden* with James Dean, *Requiem for a Heavyweight*, *Harper*, *The People Next Door*, *Reflections in a Golden Eye*, *The Hiding Place*, *The Dark Half*.

TELEVISION: *Little Moon of Alban* (Emmy Award), *Ethan Frome*, *The Lark*, *Pygmalion*, *A Doll's House*, *Victoria Regina* (Emmy Award), *The Power and the Glory*, *Johnny Belinda*, *The Christmas Wife*, and *Knot's Landing*.

Madeline Kahn

BROADWAY: *The Sisters Rosensweig*, directed by Daniel Sullivan, costumes by Jane Greenwood (Tony Award), *Born Yesterday* (Tony nomination), *On the Twentieth Century* (Tony nomination), *In the Boom Boom Room* (Tony nomination, Drama Desk Award), *Two by Two*.

OFF-BROADWAY: Donald Margulies' *What's Wrong with This Picture?* John Guare's *Marco Polo Sings a Solo*, *Promenade*.

REGIONAL: A.R. Gurney's *Love Letters*, Kafka's *Amerika*, *Blithe Spirit*.

MUSIC: *La Boheme*, *Candide* (New York Philharmonic), *La Perichole*, *She Loves Me*.

FILM: *What's Up, Doc?*, *Paper Moon* (Academy Award nomination), *Blazing Saddles* (Academy Award nomination), *Young Frankenstein* (Golden Globe nomination), *High Anxiety*, *The Adventure of Sherlock Holmes' Smarter Brother*, *Clue*, *Betsy's Wedding*.

TELEVISION: *Oh, Madeline* (People's Choice Award), *Mr. President*, *Sesame Street*, After School Special (Emmy Award), Host of *Saturday Night Live*, and George Gershwin, Irvin Berlin, and Stephen Sondheim galas.

HONORARY DEGREE: Doctor of Fine Arts, Boston Conservatory.

Terry Kinney

BROADWAY: *The Grapes of Wrath* directed by Frank Galati (Tony nomination, Best Supporting Actor)—also on the West End in London.

OFF-BROADWAY: Michael Weller's *Loose Ends*, Lyle Kessler's *Orphans*, Lanford Wilson's *Balm in Gilead*.

REGIONAL: *Sweet Bird of Youth* with Joanne Woodward and Charles Durning (Royal Alexandra, Toronto), *Tuesday's Child* (Williamstown Theatre Festival). Steppenwolf Theatre Company, Chicago (founding member): *Orphans*, *Balm in Gilead*, *Tracers*, *Death of a Salesman*, *Action*, *The House*, and many more.

FILM: *The Firm*, *The Body Snatchers*, *The Last of the Mohicans*, *Queens Logic*, *No Mercy*, *A Walk on the Moon*, *Seven Minutes in Heaven*, *Miles from Home* directed by Gary Sinise.

TELEVISION: *Deadly Matrimony*, *Murder Ordained*, *Jesse and the Bandit Queen*, *Thirtysomething*.

WORK AS DIRECTOR: *And a Nightingale Sang* (Drama Desk nomination), *Of Mice and Men*, *Fool for Love*, *Streamers*, *Servy-'N-Bernice 4 Ever*.

Marcia Jean Kurtz

BROADWAY: *Execution of Justice, Thieves,* and *The Chinese and Dr. Fish.*

OFF-BROADWAY: *When She Danced* directed by Tim Luscombe (Obie Award and Drama Desk nomination), *The Loman Family Picnic* (Obie Award), *The Last of the Red Hot Lovers, The Orphan, The Dybbuk, The Year Boston Won the Pennant, Today I Am a Fountain Pen, America Hurrah,* and *Viet Rock.*

REGIONAL: *The Workroom, Uncle Vanya, Man in the Moon Marigolds, Slow Dance on the Killing Ground, The Mirror.*

FILM: *Dog Day Afternoon, The Stoolie, Panic in Needle Park, Cold Feet, Running on Empty, Once Upon a Time in America, Deathwish, Made for Each Other.*

TELEVISION: *Law and Order, Against the Law, Gideon Oliver, The Four of Us, Date Rape, Concealed Enemies, Prisoner Without a Name, Cell Without a Number.*

Robert Sean Leonard

BROADWAY: *Candida* (Tony nomination, Best Supporting Actor), *The Speed of Darkness, Breaking the Code* with Derek Jacobi, *Brighton Beach Memoirs.*

OFF-BROADWAY: *Romeo and Juliet, When She Danced* directed by Tim Luscombe, *And the Air Didn't Answer, Sally's Gone, She Left Her Name, Coming of Age in SoHo, The Beach House* with George Grizzard.

REGIONAL: *Long Day's Journey into Night, King Lear.*

TOURS: *Biloxi Blues* and *Brighton Beach Memoirs.*

FILM: *The Age of Innocence, Much Ado about Nothing, Swing Kids, Married to It, Mr. and Mrs. Bridge, Dead Poets Society, My Best Friend Is a Vampire, The Manhattan Project.*

TELEVISION: *Bluffing It, My Two Loves, The Robert Klein Show.*

S. Epatha Merkerson

BROADWAY: *The Piano Lesson* (Tony and Drama Desk nominations), *Tintypes.*

OFF-BROADWAY: *I'm Not Stupid* (Obie Award), *Lady Day at Emerson's Bar and Grill* directed by André Ernotte, *Three Ways Home, Balm in Gilead, The Harvesting, Puppetplay, Spell #7.*

REGIONAL: *The Piano Lesson* (Helen Hayes and Los Angeles Drama Critics nominations).

FILM: *Terminator II, Jacob's Ladder, Navy Seals, Loose Cannons* and Spike Lee's *She's Gotta Have It.*

TELEVISION: *Law and Order* (series regular), *Equal Justice, Moe's World, Max and Molly, Elysian Fields, The Cosby Show, Beverly Hills Buntz,* and *PeeWee's Playhouse* (series regular).

Cynthia Nixon

BROADWAY: *The Heidi Chronicles, Hurlyburly* by David Rabe, *The Real Thing* by Tom Stoppard, *The Philadelphia Story* (Theatre World Award).

OFF-BROADWAY: Neal Bell's *On the Bum* directed by Don Scardino, *Servy-'N-Bernice 4 Ever* directed by Terry Kinney, *The Balcony Scene, Romeo and Juliet, Lemon Sky, Lydie Breeze.*

REGIONAL: *Arms and the Man, The Master Builder, Our Town, Who's Afraid of Virginia Woolf?* with Glenda Jackson and John Lithgow (Los Angeles Drama Critics' nomination).

FILM: *The Pelican Brief, Let It Ride* with Richard Dreyfuss, *The Manhattan Project, Amadeus, O.C. and Stiggs, Prince of the City, Little Darlings.*

TELEVISION: *Face of a Stranger* with Gena Rowlands, *Love, Lies and Murder, The Love She Sought* with Angela Lansbury, *Law and Order, Young Riders, Women and Wallace, Gideon Oliver, Tanner '88, The Murder of Mary Phagan* with Jack Lemmon, *It's No Crush, I'm in Love* (After school Special), Lanford Wilson's *The Fifth of July.*

Roger Rees

BROADWAY: *The Life and Adventures of Nicholas Nickleby* (Tony Award, Best Actor), *London Assurance.*

LONDON: *The Real Thing, Hapgood, Nicholas Nickleby* (Olivier Award). With the Royal Shakespeare Company: *Hamlet, Love's Labours Lost,* and *Double Double* (which he co-authored).

STRATFORD-ON-AVON: *The Three Sisters, Twelfth Night, Cymbeline, Much Ado About Nothing, Macbeth, Othello, The Merchant of Venice, The Winter's Tale, The Suicide,* etc.

LOS ANGELES: *Hapgood, Cabaret Verboten.*

FILM: Mel Brooks' *Robin Hood: Men in Tights, Star 80, Mountains of the Moon, If Looks Could Kill, Stop! or My Mom Will Shoot, Sammie and Rosie Get Laid, Do Not Disturb.*

TELEVISION: *Cheers* (series regular), *A Christmas Carol* opposite George C. Scott, *The Ebony Tower* opposite Laurence Olivier, *Nicholas Nickleby* (Emmy nomination, Best Actor), and *Young Riders.*

Associate Artist with the Royal Shakespeare Company for over twenty years, Associate Artistic Director of the Bristol Old Vic (1986–87), currently adjunct professor at UCLA.

Ron Rifkin

BROADWAY: Paddy Chayefsky's *The Tenth Man,* Neil Simon's *Come Blow Your Horn,* Herb Gardner's *The Goodbye People.*

OFF-BROADWAY: Jon Robin Baitz's *Three Hotels* (Drama Desk nomination), Jon Robin Baitz's *The Substance of Fire* (Obie Award, Drama Desk Award, Lucille Lortel Award—all for Best Actor), *Fathers, Temple,* Jerome Robbins Project-'91.

REGIONAL: *The Art of Dining,* Arthur Miller's *The American Clock,* Lanford Wilson's *Talley's Folly, Rosebloom, The Three Sisters, Ghetto, Afternoon Tea, Cross Country, Ice.*

FILM: Woody Allen's *Husbands and Wives* and *Manhattan Murder Mystery*, Oliver Stone's *JFK*, *The Sting II*, *The Sunshine Boys*, *Love Song of Charles Faberman*, *The Chosen*, *Rabbit Test*, among others.

TELEVISION: *Buying a Landslide*, *The Sunset Gang*, *Mother Courage*, *Do You Remember Love? Dress Gray*, *The Winds of War*, *The Glitter Palace*, *Evergreen*, *The Chicago Conspiracy Trial*, and a series regular on *The Trials of Rosie O'Neill*, *One Day at a Time*, *Husbands, Wives and Lovers*, *The Mary Tyler Moore Comedy Hour*, *When Things Were Rotten*, and *Adam's Rib*.

Sab Shimono

BROADWAY: *Mame*, Stephen Sondheim's *Pacific Overtures*, *Ride the Winds*, *Lovely Ladies*, *Kind Gentlemen*.

OFF-BROADWAY: Philip Kan Gotanda's *The Wash* and *Yankee Dawg You Die*, *The Music Lesson*, *Iago*, *Santa Anita*, *Chickencoop Chinaman*, *Year of the Dragon*, etc.

REGIONAL: *Fish Head Soup*, *The Winter Dances*, *The Wash* (Drama-Logue Award), *Yankee Dawg You Die*, *Macbeth*, *Iago* (Drama-Logue Award), *The Commission*, *Barbary Coast*, *Performance Anxiety* (Drama-Logue Award), *And the Soul Shall Dance*, *Avocado Kid*, *Ripples on the Pond*, etc.

FILM: *Ninja Turtles III*, *Come See the Paradise*, *Presumed Innocent*, *Barr Sinister*, *The Wash*, *Blind Date*, *Gung Ho*, *The Challenge*, *Midway*, *Puzzle of a Down Fall Child*, *Hospital*.

TELEVISION: *Hiroshima*, *And the Soul Shall Dance*, *When Hell Was in Session*, *Hot Summer Winds*, *Pueblo*, *A Year in the Life*, *How the West Was Won*, *Modesty Blaise*, *Gung Ho*, *T.H.E. Hospital*, *Remington Steele*, etc.